W9-CPH-149

the HOPE *we hold*

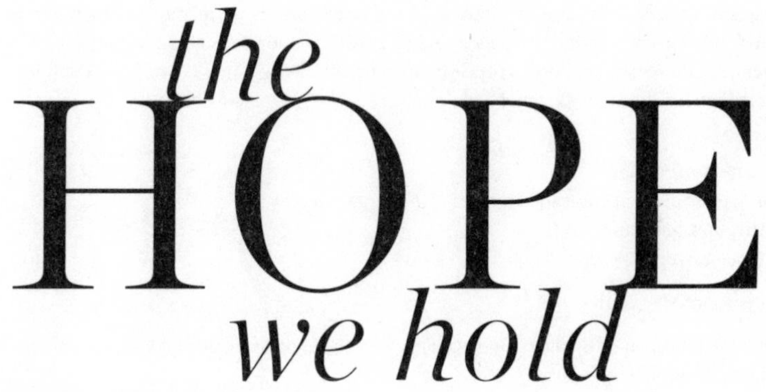

FINDING PEACE IN THE PROMISES OF GOD

Jinger & Jeremy Vuolo

with Bethany Mauger

New York • Nashville

Cover design by Michelle Lenger
Cover photograph by Russell Baer Photography

Worthy
Hachette Book Group
1290 Avenue of the Americas, New York, NY 10104
worthypublishing.com
twitter.com/worthypub

First edition: May 2021

Worthy is a division of Hachette Book Group, Inc. The Worthy name and logo are trademarks of Hachette Book Group, Inc.

The publisher is not responsible for websites (or their content) that are not owned by the publisher.

The Hachette Speakers Bureau provides a wide range of authors for speaking events. To find out more, go to www.hachettespeakersbureau.com or call (866) 376-6591.

Library of Congress Cataloging-in-Publication Data

Names: Vuolo, Jeremy, author. | Duggar, Jinger, author.
Title: The hope we hold : finding peace in the promises of God / [Jinger &] Jeremy Vuolo.
Description: First edition. | New York : Worthy, 2021.
Identifiers: LCCN 2020054029 | ISBN 9781546015857 (hardcover) | ISBN 9781546015864 (ebook)
Subjects: LCSH: Vuolo, Jeremy. | Duggar, Jinger. | Christian biography—United States. | Married people—United States—Biography. | Television personalities—United States—Biography. | Reality television programs—United States. | Hope—Religious aspects—Christianity. | Marriage—Religious aspects—Christianity. | Christian life.
Classification: LCC BR1700.3 .V86 2021 | DDC 277.94/930922 [B]—dc23
LC record available at https://lccn.loc.gov/2020054029

ISBNs: 978-1-5460-1585-7 (hardcover), 978-1-5460-1586-4 (ebook)

Printed in the United States of America

LSC-C

Printing 2, 2021

To our girls, Felicity Nicole and Evangeline Jo,
and to Halleli Grace, our little one we will meet in heaven.
We love you.

Contents

Introduction

Redefining Hope

This is a book about hope.

Technically, yes, it's our story. In the pages that follow, we'll share the details of our childhoods, how we met and fell in love, and our lives in Laredo and, now, California. Below the surface, weaving together every triumph and trial in our lives, is the silver thread of hope.

We don't mean hope the way it's often used today. You might hope you win the lottery or get a promotion at work, or that your favorite team wins the Super Bowl (go Eagles!). That kind of hope is nothing more than wishful thinking. You wouldn't bet your soul on it.

In Christ, however, we find a different definition. It's the definition we live by, the definition that carried us through the early days of knowing each other, through a mission trip in Central America when we weren't sure how the other person felt. It carried us through a long-distance relationship spanning from Springdale, Arkansas, to Laredo, Texas. It carried us through sleepless nights as new parents and a move across the country to a new home on the coast.

This hope is the reason we're happily married and genuinely delight in each other. It's the reason that, while we've had plenty of disagreements, we can honestly say we've never had a fight. It's the foundation that's held us steady through the uncertain early days of our relationship and even the loss of our unborn baby. Like a diamond that sparkles and shimmers differently in sunlight and shadows, hope might not always look the same, but it's still there, independent of our circumstances.

Make no mistake, we're not perfect. We're sinful people like anyone else, saved by a holy God. The marriage we have today and the path we walk are rooted in our hope in the person and promise of Christ. He's sovereign. He's all-powerful. He's good. He's unchanging. Other people, even our spouse, will fail us. We will fail others despite our best intentions. But the Lord never will. Because we trust Him, we can trust that He keeps his promises. When Scripture tells us He will never leave us nor forsake us, you can take that promise to the bank. The storms of life might drag us underwater, but, like a buoy in an ocean, our hope in Christ pulls us back to the surface. This is the lens through which we view life, the lens we invite you to use as you read our story.

We find this lens in the book of 1 Peter, beginning in Chapter 1. The Bible has no shortage of hopeful passages, but this is one of our favorites:

> Blessed be the God and Father of our Lord Jesus Christ! According to his great mercy, he has caused us to be born again to a living hope through the resurrection of Jesus Christ from the dead, to an inheritance that is imperishable, undefiled, and unfading, kept in heaven for you, who by God's power are being guarded through faith for a salvation ready to be revealed in the last time. In this you rejoice, though now for a little while, if necessary, you have been grieved by various trials, so that the tested genuineness of your faith—more precious than gold that perishes though it is tested by fire—may be found to result in praise and glory and

> honor at the revelation of Jesus Christ. Though you have not seen him, you love him. Though you do not now see him, you believe in him and rejoice with joy that is inexpressible and filled with glory, obtaining the outcome of your faith, the salvation of your souls. (1 Peter 1:3–9 ESV)

These words are nothing short of a miracle. Even when we were trapped in the muck and mire of our sin, the Lord showed us mercy—not just any mercy, but *great* mercy. God chose to transform us through the life, death, and resurrection of Jesus Christ, and He didn't stop there. He promises that those who believe can look forward to an inheritance in Him. We have everything to gain in glory, and nobody can touch that or take it away.

This hope doesn't mean we're protected from trials. In fact, this passage warns that we will endure grief and struggle. But even in our grief, we can be confident that our trials aren't for nothing. Each trial is a fire that purifies our faith, refining us, bringing us into God's glory. We can rest in this promise, thanking God in the trial, and even asking Him how we can glorify Him. These words are a balm to the aching soul. God is not only with you in the fire, but He promises to carry you to the other side as new creation. This is the ultimate hope that transformed our lives, that's available to all who accept it.

We're about to share with you our highest highs and our very lowest lows. We're getting vulnerable with you because we want you to see the hope of Christ woven through our story. It hasn't always looked the same. Like a diamond sparkles differently in the light and shadows, it's still true, still shining, whether we're on the mountaintop or deep in the valley.

This isn't a how-to guide for life or marriage. We don't pretend to have all the answers. As Peter said to the lame man in Acts 3, we have no silver or gold, but what we do have, we give to you. There is hope in Christ for every person, every marriage, every walk of life. There is an inheritance of glory, a life richer than you can imagine, if you only walk with the Lord.

Chapter One

Going with the Flow

Jinger

The questions always came. They came during trips to Aldi, or as we licked our dollar ice cream cones at the Springdale, Arkansas, McDonald's.

I could feel the eyes of strangers on us as my siblings and I trailed behind my mom like little ducklings on the sidewalk. Finally, somebody would work up the courage to approach us.

"Are these *all* your kids?" they'd ask incredulously, drawing out the word "all." "How do you do all that laundry?"

"How do you cook for so many people?"

"How many bathrooms do you have?"

Sometimes, they'd turn to me. "Do you like having all these brothers and sisters?"

The questions didn't bother me. I was used to the intrusion. Besides, I couldn't blame them for noticing us. My childhood wasn't exactly what you'd call normal—not by the rest of the world's standards, anyway. By the time I was born, my family was already larger than most. I was baby number six in the Duggar family, sandwiched between my big sister of thirteen months, Jessa, and my brother Joseph, who was born about a year later.

Every year or two, my parents, Jim Bob and Michelle Duggar, announced a new brother or sister was on the way. We saw each one as a blessing, and every baby was greeted with the same squeals of excitement, whether it was baby number nine or nineteen.

In my eyes, a family our size was nothing out of the ordinary. Mom and Dad had decided to welcome as many babies as the Lord gave them, and most of our friends had the same philosophy. Each week at church, we were surrounded by families with eight or more children. In my child-like eyes, I accepted what I saw before me as normal. Who wouldn't like living with a house full of playmates?

I was happy in our home. It was noisy and bustling with activity from morning until late at night, and I loved it that way. Somebody was always around to play kickball in the backyard or go bargain hunting at the local thrift shop. Somebody was always there to listen to my secrets or giggle over a new joke I'd heard. Somebody was always up for picking apples or cherries from our backyard trees or playing with trucks on the giant dirt pile outside.

Running off and doing your own thing wasn't an option most of the time in our 2,000-square-foot, three-bedroom house. That was OK with me. My siblings and I preferred to be together anyway. Our parents set us up dormitory style on blue and red metal bunk beds, with all the girls in one room, all the boys in another. While we gravitated toward the siblings around our own ages, I felt close to each brother and sister. Jessa, especially, was my best friend from day one. People often mistook us for twins, as we were just one year apart and looked quite similar, and sometimes, we liked to imagine that was true. We loved dressing alike and whispering in our bunk beds long after the lights were out for the night.

It's a good thing we kids enjoyed one another. Most days, there was no escaping my siblings. Mom homeschooled us, we sat side by side during our daily Bible study and prayer, and we even took piano and violin lessons together. With so many people living in our house, I learned quickly to go with the flow, to be the family peacemaker. I didn't like getting into trouble and wanted to please Mom and Dad. Not that I never found my way into mischief. Jessa was the more headstrong one between the two of us—ask her, she'd tell you so herself!—and she always told me or Joseph to pull somebody's hair or play a prank that inevitably led to trouble.

From the beginning, Mom and Dad realized they couldn't run our household as referees. They taught us that we need to think of others before ourselves. "It's not all about you," they must have said a thousand times. "The world does not revolve around you." I heard those words when we battled for seats near the air conditioner in our fifteen-passenger van, or when I complained that somebody pulled my hair or sat on my bed. "You need to talk sweetly to your sister," they'd say. "Be patient with each other."

I learned what patience looked like by watching Mom. As loud and chaotic as we could be, I don't ever remember her yelling or even raising her voice. In a house full of kids, she was our calming force, our rock. We knew we could come to her with any problem and we'd have her full attention. "Do you want to stop and pray about that right now?" she asked every time. "You pray first, and I'll go after you." Mom didn't always have the answers, but she pointed us to the one who did. Even today, she regularly prays with me over the phone when I bring her a concern or problem.

Mom and Dad went out of their way to make sure none of us kids felt lost in the shuffle. Somehow, they managed to give us one-on-one attention, whether that meant my dad bringing one of us to work or

Mom letting us tag along on a trip to the bank. I leaned back in the car seat and chattered away to them about the latest game my sisters and I were playing or a boy who caught my eye. I never doubted that my parents truly knew me and my heart, that they loved me, that they thought I was special.

If Mom and Dad weren't available, Grandma Duggar was there. She and Grandpa stopped by our house almost every day, and if Mom and Dad needed a date night, they would come over and watch us. If I was craving ice cream, I could count on her to be up for a quick trip to Braum's for a cone. We Duggars are known for our bargain shopping, but it was Grandma Duggar who taught me the tricks of the trade. She knew all the best places to find cute clothes for incredible deals, and she had an eye for outfits with potential that other people might have overlooked. And there was no ripped seam or torn skirt that she couldn't fix. I felt grown-up as she handed me a needle of my own, showing me how to fit the thread through the tiny eye and sew on a button so it wouldn't fall off again. Grandma Duggar was tough, with a strong personality, but that was one of the reasons I loved her so much.

On weekdays, Mom ran our house like a well-oiled machine. Our daily schedules were carefully organized and displayed on the kitchen wall with color-coded Post-it Notes. Each day tended to start on the later side—my parents were night owls, and the rest of us followed suit. We preferred staying up late playing, and we always waited until the last minute to sneak in our required minutes of violin and piano practice. Every once in a while, Mom declared we had to get on an earlier schedule and stop staying up so late. They would wake us up at the crack of dawn, sometimes even carrying us to the breakfast table wrapped in our comforters. Inevitably, though, we slipped back into our later routine.

Getting up early had its advantages. Since we were homeschooled, we could work at our own pace. If you finished your lessons for the day early enough, you could hop in the van with Dad and go with him to scout out real estate properties or work on any number of his house projects. Anyone who stayed home could play at the Christian school playground next door, across a cow field.

Everyone was expected to help out around the house, with each person having assigned chores, which my parents called our "jurisdictions." Somebody cleaned the girls' room and boys' room, someone was assigned the bathrooms, someone helped stock the pantry, and on and on. My favorite jurisdiction was laundry. As big a job as it was, I liked the challenge of getting it all done as quickly as I could. Grandma Duggar, who was a constant presence in our home, helped me throw loads into our four washing machines, and a sweet woman from church visited twice a week to help us fold and put away clothing. I loved going through the family clothes, tossing what was too worn out to use, and organizing the rest in the family closet in the laundry room, where all the kids' clothes were kept. It made more sense to keep everything together in one big room, since some of us wore the same sizes and neither bedroom was big enough for each of us to have a closet. By the time I was finished putting everything away, I felt a surge of pride, like I'd truly accomplished something great.

Feeding a family our size required a massive pantry stocked like a grocery storeroom. Our trips to Aldi required all hands on deck to load flats of canned food into cart after cart, and our final tab regularly topped $800. As kids, we thought nothing of opening up a can of green beans or beef ravioli and eating it as a snack, straight from the can at room temperature.

Once, Dad encouraged Mom to head out of town for a women's conference. "Don't you worry about us, Michelle," he assured her. "I can handle the kids. You go and enjoy yourself."

Mom stocked the deep freezer full of meals before she left and even wrote out instructions for how each one should be prepared. Dad wasn't much of a cook, and most of us kids were too young to help him.

But if Dad knew about those meals, he didn't let on. When Dad called us to dinner that first night, there wasn't the familiar scent of a casserole bubbling away in the oven or meat simmering in a Crock-Pot. We sat down at the table to find cans of lima beans, corn, green beans, and potatoes sitting in front of us. Dad stood up with a can opener, cracking open the cans and pouring the cold, undrained contents on our plates. I stared at the unappetizing mound in front of me. I may have been used to cold canned food, but I drew the line at lima beans.

"Oh wait, you guys need some protein too," Dad said, walking back to the pantry. A moment later, he appeared with cans of tuna, a bag of bread, and a bottle of barbecue sauce. I watched in horror as he spread barbecue sauce on slices of bread and slapped pieces of tuna fish between them.

"Here you go," he said, as he handed out his creation. I shrugged. If I had to choose between barbecue tuna fish sandwiches or cold lima beans, the lesser of the two evils was obvious. I sucked in my breath, closed my eyes, and took a bite.

"Hey, this is good!" I said with surprise. My brothers and sisters nodded enthusiastically. A chorus of "Mmm!" and "Yum!" broke out around the table.

The reviews were unanimous. Dad nearly burst with pride at having created a new favorite meal. He couldn't wait to tell my mom that she had a new recipe to add to the rotation. To this day, I'll open a can of tuna and drizzle it with barbecue sauce for a snack. It's still delicious.

On weekends, sometimes Dad yelled, "OK, everybody load up in the van!" We buckled our seat belts and took off, driving for what felt like hours but in reality was probably only a few minutes. Sometimes, we ended up at a park or an ice cream parlor. Most of the time, we stopped at a house or property along the way. Dad worked in real estate and couldn't resist the opportunity to check out a new prospect. Looking back, I realize those drives were his way of including the family even when he had work to do. He didn't want to choose between being with us and working hard enough to support us all, so he found a way to do both. To us kids, those drives weren't work. They were an adventure, with a world full of possibilities ahead of us.

• • •

I was still a little girl when Dad was elected to the Arkansas House of Representatives. The legislature met in Little Rock, about three hours away from our home in Springdale. Most other state legislators kept apartments in the capital city and drove home on weekends when the legislature was in session. That wasn't an option for Dad. He didn't want to be away from us that long if he could help it.

Instead, we all headed to Little Rock with him. We rented a house and kept up our homeschool studies and music lessons. Sometimes, Dad took one or two of us along to the Capitol Building with him. I felt breathless as I held his hand and stepped into the white domed building where our state's laws were made. I stood next to Dad on the House floor as representatives voted and the Speaker banged the gavel. Every once in a while, I looked around the semicircular room at the high ceilings and ornate pillars surrounding me and sighed, completely in awe of its beauty.

Given the nature of Dad's position, he was often invited to political banquets, rallies, and Lincoln Day dinners. Usually, that invitation included his family too. Of course, he didn't bring the whole family, but would take the older set along while the younger kids stayed home with Grandma and Grandpa Duggar. Just who was included in the older set depended on who showed enough growth and maturity to sit with Mom and Dad without getting restless. For the longest time, only Josh, Jana, John-David, and Jill were invited along. As much as we loved those evenings with Grandma and Grandpa, Jessa and I sat at home dreaming of donning our fanciest dresses and elegantly choosing the right fork at the same table with the older kids.

We always assumed Jessa would be ushered into the older set first. She wasn't older by much, but she had me beat by thirteen months. So, when Mom and Dad invited both of us to a Lincoln Day dinner, I felt Jessa tense up.

"Jinge is coming too?" she asked.

I braced myself. She didn't say the word "already," but she didn't have to. I knew Jessa had waited longer than she wanted to be considered part of the older set. Jessa was the tomboy of tomboys, while our next oldest sister, Jill, was remarkably calm and composed and never even scuffed her shoes. My go-with-the-flow tendencies demonstrated themselves as maturity, so we were both invited to join the older crowd.

If she couldn't beat me into the older set, Jessa decided to make the best of it. We were still the best of friends, and we relished picking out matching homemade dresses and bows for the occasion. Whether we got there separately or together, we were the older kids now.

Dad had served a couple of terms in the Arkansas legislature when he decided to run for the US Senate. I wondered if we'd move to Washington, D.C., but it turned out, I didn't need to worry. Dad's run wasn't successful. I figured our lives would go back to normal now, that we'd return to Springdale full-time and pick up right where we left off. The Lord, however, had other plans.

You see, on Election Day, my dad brought the whole family to the polling location, just like he always had for his previous runs, and a photographer from the Associated Press snapped a picture of all fourteen of us kids trailing behind him at the voting booth. Somehow, that picture found its way into the hands of someone at *Parents* magazine. That led to Mom writing a short article about our family, explaining how she ran our household of fourteen kids and sharing our faith. All of us huddled around the glossy magazine when it arrived, excited to see our names in print. I thought it was cool to see our family in a real magazine, but we all thought that would be the end of it.

It wasn't long before Mom and Dad sat us down in the living room for a family meeting. I knew something was up. A family meeting always meant big news, usually a new baby on the way. They had also sat us down like this to tell us Dad would be running for office. So, I wasn't expecting the words that came out of Dad's mouth next.

"Guys, listen up," he said, quieting us down. "A TV channel has asked to do a documentary about our family. It's called Discovery Health."

I looked around at my brothers and sisters, my eyes wide. My ten-year-old mind could barely comprehend my dad's words. I had never seen a TV show beyond animated Bible stories and Lowe's home improvement videos. Our family TV didn't even sit in our living room. My parents stored it in a closet, only to be hauled out for special occasions, like a major news event. The idea of being on TV myself was completely foreign.

"We need to pray about this," Mom said seriously. "This is a big decision."

In the end, my parents said yes. Discovery Health sent them a couple of documentaries they'd done in the past—*Mysteries of Cold Water Survival* and *Joined for Life*. Mom and Dad felt peace of mind after watching those documentaries and believed the channel would handle our story well. And, as a bonus, those DVDs were now approved by Mom and Dad. We watched them so many times we practically had them memorized.

My parents had one condition for Discovery Health. They didn't want the documentary to edit out our faith.

"It's your story," the channel executive told my dad. "We'll let you tell it."

• • •

The first thing I noticed were the cameras. A line of men on our doorstep carried giant black boxes on their shoulders so big I wondered for a moment if they might fall over. My eyes followed the cameras to the thick cables connected to them, running to the boom microphones held by still more crew members.

We'd spent countless hours dreaming of this moment, wondering what the crew would be like, and practicing our most polite greetings. We slicked back our unruly chestnut curls and slid into matching homemade clothes—plaid dresses for the girls and polo shirts for the boys. We were so excited we hardly slept the night before the big first day of filming.

Now that the camera crew was here, everything I'd practiced in my head suddenly disappeared. I stared at the man before me, drawing a complete blank. I remembered the words my parents had coached me to say in the nick of time. I looked the cameraman in the eye and smiled. "Hello, my name is Jinger," I said, hoping my voice didn't shake too badly. "It's nice to meet you."

The man smiled back. "I'm Scott Enlow," he said. "I'll be shooting the documentary."

The documentary. Even with the cameras in the house, it still hardly seemed real. We were a normal family, with nothing particularly special about us. Why would somebody want to put us on TV?

Scott warned that while they might ask us to do something several times, like walk through a door over and over, he wanted us to act natural. "Be yourselves," he told us. "Don't look at the camera. Act like we're not here."

Those words were much easier said than done. How was I supposed to not look at the massive equipment filling up our whole living room, or at these strangers I'd never met?

I could feel my knees shaking as crew members Kirk and Deanie lined us up in the living room by our birth order. All we had to do was smile and say our name, they told us. This seemingly simple task suddenly seemed incredibly daunting. I practiced the words in my head over and over until it was my turn. *I'm Jinger Duggar. I'm Jinger Duggar.*

I breathed a sigh of relief when the words came out as I practiced them. My little brother Jedidiah wasn't so lucky.

"I'm Josiah—Jedidiah Duggar," he stammered. We still tease him today about the moment he was so nervous he forgot his own name.

My eyes wandered toward the camera that followed us as we loaded the washing machine and fixed tater tot casserole for that night's dinner. The crew recorded us playing kickball in the backyard and sat us down for interviews on our bunk beds. In between takes, they let us play with the boom microphones and try on their headphones. One of the sound men, Dee, was so tall that we begged him to try to touch the top of our highest doorway. Slowly, we forgot about the cameras. Scott and the crew became new playmates to us, people we were thrilled to have in our home. By the time the crew packed up and left for the day, I was on cloud nine. I'm sure Mom and Dad were exhausted, but I couldn't have been more excited.

The crew visited our house a few more times over the course of several months. They were there when we learned baby number fifteen was a boy, and when we met little Jackson for the first time. When we all said goodbye after their last visit, I felt like we were saying goodbye to family. *I wonder if we'll ever see them again*, I thought.

• • •

My heart pounded when Mom and Dad showed us the DVD they'd received from Discovery Health a few months later. Our documentary, *14 Children and Pregnant Again!*, was finished. As long as we gave our approval, it would air on Discovery Health. The whole world would see our family, our house, how we lived.

I wasn't sure if I was more nervous or excited as Dad popped the DVD into the player. As soon as our images appeared on the screen, any nerves I might have had disappeared. I grinned so hard my cheeks hurt as I watched myself, my siblings, and my parents on the screen. Sitting in my living room and watching our lives on a TV show was surreal and incredible all at once. By the time the credits rolled, we all agreed it was adorable and absolutely perfect.

Even if no one watches it but us, I'll remember this as long as I live, I thought. I figured this was a fun chapter of our lives that was over now. I didn't realize it was only the beginning.

Chapter Two

Pastor's Son

Jeremy

The hallway was dark as I crept out of my room. I could hear my older brother, Chuck, roll over in his bed, the creaking floor interrupting his deep slumber for a brief moment.

I was only five years old, but my conscience was on fire. Maybe it was the sermon my dad had preached that morning, or the gospel message my Sunday school teacher shared with my class before church. Whatever it was, I didn't want to live in my sin for another moment, even if it was eleven o'clock at night.

My parents had already turned out their light when I opened their bedroom door. "Dad?" I whispered, tapping him on his shoulder.

"Jeremy?" Dad was always especially exhausted on Sundays, his mind and body spent after a day of preaching and ministering to his congregation. "What's wrong, son?"

I searched for the words to explain my feelings, to make them understand the overwhelming concern for my soul that kept my eyes open long past my bedtime. Finally, I said simply, "I want to know Jesus."

Dad scooped me onto the bed and sat me between him and Mom.

I could hardly wait to pray and ask Jesus to save me from my sin. They prayed with me, and my parents now tell me they saw an immediate change in me. Where before they had seen deep concern and alarm, they could now see relief wash over me. I was so happy that I wanted to get what I called my bug-eyed Bible—which was really a children's Bible with large-eyed animated characters—and make up a song to celebrate. I made up a song to the tune of the *Barney and Friends* theme song: "I love God, he loves me, I'm as free as I can be, 'cause he took my sins and nailed them to the tree, I love God and he loves me!" It seems cheesy as I look back on that moment, but at the time, the joy in my heart was real, and I had to show it somehow.

"Jeremy, you're part of Jesus' family," my dad told me.

From the beginning, my parents provided me with a godly example. My mom, Diana, was a professional violinist who had recently been saved when she met my dad, Chuck, who served Cambodian refugees at an inner-city church in North Philadelphia. They fell in love, got married, and had two other children, Chuck and Val, before they had me.

I grew up to the sounds of violins and Bible verses, symphonies and sermons. At home, Mom played so much Beethoven and Tchaikovsky that if I heard a few notes from one of their symphonies today, I could probably hum the rest. On Sundays, my siblings and I crowded next to my mom in the pews of The Reformed Baptist Church of Downingtown while Dad preached.

Dad made it clear that serving Christ wasn't about putting on a show each Sunday morning, and he meant it. My parents loved a very real God who impacted how they lived, how they talked, how they interacted with others. Even in the varying circumstances of ministry, they always responded with humility and grace, even when he was wrongly criticized.

Once, my dad returned home from hours of meetings with church members, his face calm and composed.

"Dad, why aren't you angry?" I asked him, flabbergasted. "Why don't you say something to them?"

Dad shook his head. "Son, I need to examine my heart first. I need to seek the Lord and see if what they're saying is true."

My mouth gaped open. Not only was my dad not angry, but he was also gracious and even kind. I couldn't understand it. I sure didn't have that kind of self-control. I wondered if I ever would.

Our family lived about half a mile from the church in a little brick two-story house on a corner lot. I grew up ducking in a holly bush on the side of the house during games of hide-and-seek and sneaking into my tree fort that served as my imaginary blacksmith shop, hammering away at spoons I borrowed from our kitchen. I like to think of myself back then as an energetic, fun-loving kid. Others might have called me hyperactive.

My dad's church felt like our second home, considering the amount of time we spent there. Chuck, Val, and I roamed the pews and played tag in the churchyard long after the last parishioner had left a Sunday morning service or Wednesday night prayer meeting. Sometimes, Dad brought us to the church to play while he studied for his upcoming sermon. A soccer field sat outside the church, and Val and I liked to kick the soccer ball around whenever we had the chance.

Val and I were on the field one evening as a team using the other half of the field ended its practice. I turned from the goal to see three boys walking with their dad toward us. They were strangers to me, but later, I'd learn they were triplets named Mark, Mike, and Keith Lesch. I wiped the sweat from my forehead and watched them approaching me, wondering what they wanted. I knew from their uniforms that the brothers played travel soccer, something I'd wanted to do too. I was only eight years old though. Mom and Dad said I wasn't ready for a travel league yet.

"Hey!" Mike called out to me. "Our team's having a tryout tomorrow night if you want to come."

All I said was, "OK." But something sparked inside me. For reasons I couldn't explain, that simple, offhand invitation sounded irresistibly appealing. I sprinted to my dad's office as fast as my legs could carry me and burst through his door, gasping for air.

"Dad!" I shouted between breaths. "They're having tryouts tomorrow. Can I go? Please?"

Dad looked up from his sermon notes and raised his eyebrows. "Who's having a tryout?"

I paced around his office with excitement, talking as I walked. "It's a travel soccer league," I explained. "And they said I could try out tomorrow if I want to."

"OK, OK." Dad held up his hand, trying to stop the constant flow of words tumbling from my mouth. "We'll check it out."

I showed up the next day in my cleats and shin guards, confident beyond my ability. I really wanted to be a goalkeeper, even though the team was an age bracket above me, but I tried out as a field player too, just in case.

It turned out I didn't make the A team, but they gave me a slot on a B team called the Mako Attack, named for an incredibly fast species of sharks. Each weekend, I showed up for morning practice, the weather cold and brisk, the air thick with the smell of freshly mowed grass. I tightened my cleat laces, now wet with dew, and kicked around the ball. Every touch of the ball against my cleats, every crunch of grass under my feet, was magical. This was only a youth travel soccer team, and not even the top team, and yet it was quickly becoming my all-consuming passion. I was only eight years old, but I knew I wanted to be a professional soccer player.

Many kids say they want to play sports professionally, but I meant it completely. I remember a church deacon looking right at me and saying, "Jeremy, you're not going to be a professional soccer player. Very few guys actually make it." The guy was probably three feet taller than me, but I stared at him, thinking, *I'm going to be one of those guys*. Even as a kid, I didn't see the point of playing if you didn't want to go pro. This wasn't about entertainment for me. This was an insatiable desire to be the best. I called myself disciplined, but obsessed might be a better word. By the time I was twelve years old, I set my alarm for 5:45 each morning. I didn't care if it was raining or snowing, I still tied on my cleats, zipped up my jacket, and spent over an hour running technical drills in my backyard. I wore the grass down to nothing but dirt. I never felt like I'd trained enough. Every morning, I didn't stop until I'd beaten my previous days' record for how many consecutive juggles—left foot only, right foot only, both feet, head, and thigh. I recorded my juggles on a sheet of paper. Before long, I could count my juggles by the thousand.

Since I was homeschooled, I finished my work as quickly as I could so I could get back out in the yard and practice. Then I sat around, anxiously biting my nails until 3:00 p.m., when my buddy Pat Powers got out of public school. I called him as soon as I thought he was home and asked him to come over and practice with me. Pat definitely contributed to the dirt patch I cultivated in the yard.

My parents set one limit to make sure our family priorities placed God first: I could practice all I wanted and play in travel leagues, but I couldn't play games on Sundays. I didn't argue with them. I wanted to honor the Lord too. That limit came with a price though. I didn't make some of the best teams because the big tournaments were always held on Saturdays and Sundays. If it came down to me and one other guy in tryouts, the coach went with the guy who was available all the time. That stung, but it also motivated me. I knew that if I couldn't play Sundays, I had to work that much harder and be that much better than everyone else.

Even though I was committed to the Lord, by the time I was fourteen, I found myself staring at the ceiling above me at night, my mind racing with questions. *Do I really love Jesus?* I wondered. *Or do I just know the right answers?* I believed that the Lord had done a work in my heart at age five, but I was different now. I was older, with the hormones and temptations that went with my age. Friends on my soccer team had already turned from the Lord, and that left me with questions, especially one that haunted me most of all: *Lord, if I died right now, would I go to heaven?*

When these questions came up, I should have done exactly what I'd done at five years old, when I walked straight to Mom and Dad's room and poured out my concern for my soul. Instead, I stuffed those questions deep inside. I told myself that if anyone found out that I wasn't even sure if I would go to heaven, I'd make my dad look bad. He was the pastor, and I didn't want my immaturities and sin to discredit him.

I kept my struggles buried inside, even as I felt less and less secure in my eternal destiny. Meanwhile, I was a teenager surrounded by kids who didn't worry about what God thought and didn't wrestle with the same internal struggles I did. I was torn between genuinely wanting to honor God and just going along with everyone around me. As I enjoyed success on the soccer field, my social circles expanded. By the end of my sophomore year, I thought my life couldn't get better. I had a reputation as a dominant goalkeeper, I was days away from turning sixteen and getting my driver's license, and my parents had even agreed to let me attend public school the upcoming year. I felt confident. A bit overconfident.

Maybe that's why I made the less-than-brilliant decision to throw a party for the soccer team while my parents were out of town. We told our families we were having a preseason get-together at my house, which wasn't unusual for our team. But we didn't mention the beer one friend supplied and the girls we invited.

I cleaned up after the party and thought I hadn't left behind a trace of the mess. Mom, it turned out, was a better detective than I suspected. Later, she told me she noticed the sofa pillows were arranged carefully, yet not like she typically arranged them, and that when she went on the deck, she noticed the sun glinting on a tiny piece of broken glass that could only have come from a beer bottle.

"What girls were here?" she asked bluntly.

I was busted. My parents, disappointed that I'd gone behind their backs, decided I wasn't prepared to jump into public school with a driver's license. What crushed me more than anything else was the look of disappointment on their faces.

"Jeremy," Mom said gently but firmly, "you've been dishonest. You've let deceit grow in your heart."

For the second time in my life, I felt the full weight of my sin. "I know, Mom." I didn't break down crying often, but in that moment, I felt tears well up in my eyes. "I want you to be able to trust me, I really do."

My dad sat by my side as I cried out to the Lord, just as he had when I was five years old. I wanted to follow Him. I saw where my pride and deceit could lead me, and I didn't want to go there again.

But then came my last year of high school. I was finally allowed to attend public school for the first time, and I was the star goalkeeper of the soccer team. My status as the new guy and an athlete brought with it a popularity I never experienced before. Kids wanted to hang out with me, and party invitations came fast and furious. I'd be lying if I said it didn't go to my head.

I told myself I was done with partying when I started my freshman year at Hartwick College. I wanted to make a difference for the Lord and focus on soccer. I couldn't do any of that if I got drunk every weekend.

The right approach would have been to stay home from parties and focus on how I could make an impact for Christ on my campus. But I didn't do that. Instead, I joined my soccer buddies at party after party, the whole time thinking, *I'm not gonna drink, I'm only going to hang out with the guys*. I might as well have walked to the edge of a cliff and hoped I didn't fall. Inevitably, I gave in to one beer, which led to another, and another, until I lost count. I woke up the next morning hungover, again and again.

You idiot, I yelled at myself in my head. *Why did you do that again?* I sometimes went to church on Sundays so hungover that I vomited in the bathroom, and I promised to do better. And for a few weeks, I did. But it was never long before I eventually gave in again.

The same scenario played out week after week, party after party, hangover after hangover. Lather, rinse, repeat. From the outside, it looked like I was having the time of my life, but the truth was, I was miserable. I couldn't even enjoy the parties because I was so racked with guilt. *I don't want to do this*, I prayed. *Why do I keep going back to my sin?*

The problem was getting worse. The parties were becoming more frequent, the drinks becoming harder. I felt myself becoming distant from my parents as I left out large chunks of my college experience while I talked to them on the phone. I never outright lied to them about what I did, I simply didn't open up about it. They assumed the best.

When I told Mom and Dad I was returning to Hartwick for a January term over winter break, I left out a few details. They knew I could knock out an entire class in a few weeks. What they didn't know was that J-Term was notorious for constant partying.

One Tuesday night during J-Term, I'd finished class for the day—I can't even remember what the topic was anymore. A buddy invited me to play beer pong and hang out with a few friends at his apartment. At first, I said no. I was tired, and I knew I should get rest. When my friend wouldn't take no for an answer, I gave in.

After a few hours, my friends had the brilliant idea to head to a bar. We drank a few cheap beers before walking to the pizza place next door after last call. We were about to head home when I noticed a guy staring at one of the girls in our group. I didn't like it. And in my inebriated state, I caught a sudden case of beer muscles.

I stared the guy down until he glared at me, jerking up his chin. "What's up?" he yelled, daring me to say something.

"C'mon, man," my buddy said quietly. "Forget this dude. Let's go."

"No." I brushed him off. "I wanna see what's up with this guy."

"Bro, it's not worth it," he said. "But if you wanna stay, I got your back."

Cold air stung my cheeks as I pushed the front door open and walked outside, the stranger right on my heels. I whipped around to face him. "You got a problem?" I snapped.

"Yeah. I got a problem." The guy was in my face now.

Adrenaline coursed through my body as we squared up, two of them, two of us. I was furious. The beers I drank that night turned me into a macho version of myself I didn't recognize. I was the tough guy, the guy who wouldn't back down, the guy who refused to look weak no matter the cost.

I noticed a police cruiser out of the corner of my eye as tensions rose. The cruiser kept driving and turned down the street. My buddy was next to me now, shouting and throwing himself into the mix.

Someone threw a punch, and the verbal altercation turned into a fight. By now, people inside the pizza joint had rushed outside to watch, like a cliché from a bad teenage movie. Time moved in slow motion as I watched the guy's fist crash into my buddy's nose. Blood poured from his nostrils as he tumbled to the ground. He was out cold.

The other guy and his friend took off running right as the police cruiser returned. This time, the officers slowed to a stop. My stomach churned as two policemen climbed out of the car and jumped in front of us.

The first officer rushed to my buddy, making sure he was OK. I think the second officer actually thought I was trying to break up the fight—which I wasn't—but for some unknown reason, I yelled at him. I'm not sure what I said. It certainly wasn't, "Hey, you're a great public servant!"

"Sir, please leave the scene," the officer said firmly, trying to clear the area.

"I ain't going anywhere," was my eloquent response. I reached over and grabbed the officer's arm. Big mistake. In a flash, the officer's hands were on my arms. I felt my face slam against the police cruiser, the metal freezing cold against my cheek. I heard something clink and felt handcuffs tighten around my wrists.

I saw the crowd staring at me, all of them wondering what kind of idiot grabs a cop. And then, my eyes fell on something else. A familiar face, someone I recognized from church. He stood in the back of the pizza place, spreading sauce on a pan of dough. For a split second, he looked up and caught my eye.

Immediately my face flushed with shame. This man was a Christian. He wasn't acting a fool or embarrassing himself like I was. He was faithfully serving the Lord. He knew I went to church too. And now, he saw me for the hypocrite I was in the worst moment of my life. I felt exposed and guilty.

• • •

Hours later, I sat in a drunk tank. I heard another drunk snoring in the cell next to me, but I couldn't sleep. Not on that hard bench, surrounded by metal bars. I sat with my head in my hands, already feeling the sickening nausea of a wicked hangover coming on. *I'm such a fool*, I thought. *What have I done?*

I thought of all the people I'd have to confess to—my coach, my pastor. I wondered how I'd pay the fine I was sure to be charged, and what I'd do if I was charged with assault. The sin I allowed in my life led me to a place so dark I had no idea how to escape. There was no way out. Not on my own.

God, I cried out in prayer. *I'm done. I can't do this anymore. I don't want to live for myself anymore. I want to live for you. I'm not going to do the Christian life halfway anymore.* I knew I either had to live for Christ or live for myself. But I couldn't call myself a Christian and live like this.

• • •

Months later, I sat in front of my computer. The cursor flashed on the e-mail I'd written to the entire Hartwick College campus from my college account. I couldn't take my eyes off the first sentence I'd written: "My name is Jeremy Vuolo, and I am a Christian."

The night of my arrest, I decided things would change. I had been lucky to avoid an assault charge and was sentenced to community service, which I completed willingly. I confessed what I'd done to my coaches, and I'd started to meet regularly with a local pastor who'd agreed to disciple me.

"Jeremy, one of the best means of accountability for you is to be outspoken as a Christian," the pastor had told me. "It's easy to give in to sin if your testimony isn't out there."

I took his advice to heart and decided to start a chapter of the Fellowship of Christian Athletes at Hartwick. I was sending an e-mail out to my fellow students to let them know about our first meeting. Now, though, my heart pounded as I imagined people around campus reading my e-mail. "Wait, isn't this the guy I saw get arrested?" I pictured them saying. "Isn't this the guy who gets trashed at parties?" As soon as I hit send, I'd be going public as a Christian—one who had certainly not walked the walk.

I closed my eyes and took a deep breath, slowly exhaling. This was my chance to get serious about serving the Lord, even if it meant humbling myself. Before I could think about it further, I hit send. My testimony was out in the world. There was no going back now.

Chapter Three

In the Public Eye

Jinger

"Wait. What's a reality show?"

I looked around at my brothers and sisters, wondering if anyone else was as confused as I was. The tilted heads and twisted faces around the living room told me no one had a clue what those words meant.

It was 2008, and my dad called all of us kids to the living room for a family meeting. I expected his big news to be that TLC was making another documentary about our family. When our first special became one of Discovery Health's top-rated shows, they asked us to make three more. *On the Road with 16 Children* detailed a cross-country trip our family took, *16 Children and Moving In* showed us putting the finishing touches on and moving into the house we'd had custom built to meet the unique needs of a family our size, and *Raising 16 Children* showed how my parents managed it all. By now, I didn't mind the cameras, and the crew members felt like old friends. I smiled as I thought of seeing Scott, Deanie, and Kirk again.

But it wouldn't be another documentary this time, Dad said. TLC didn't want to make another one-hour special. This time, the network wanted to make a reality show about our family.

All of us stared at Dad as if he had suddenly started speaking a foreign language. The rest of America was quite familiar with reality shows by this point in time, but I didn't generally watch TV. Our family's television continued to gather dust in a closet somewhere. Still, I could tell that whatever this was, it was a big deal.

"How is a show different from what we've already done?" one of my brothers asked.

Dad, who didn't exactly watch much TV himself, took a moment before he answered. "Well, the shows will be a lot more frequent," he said. "We'll have cameras in our house more often. The way I understand it, we won't be doing anything special when the crew comes. They'll follow us around while we do whatever it is we have planned for the day."

"We need to pray about it," my mom added. "We need to make sure the filming won't interrupt our daily life or work."

"But we also believe this is an opportunity." Dad looked around the living room, making eye contact with each of us. "We have a chance to tell the world about Christ right in their living rooms, all because somebody wants to give us a television show."

TLC named our show *17 Kids and Counting*—a name that changed a few times as we welcomed new babies into the family. We smiled and greeted Scott and the crew with hugs as they set up cameras and boom microphones. Then, the cameras followed us as we built a garden in the backyard or the boys worked on a truck. It seemed easy enough, especially since no one had to tell me over and over again not to look at the camera. I thought maybe a reality show wouldn't change our lives so much, given that we had already been on television.

Nothing could have prepared me for the floodgates that flew open when the show began to air. Suddenly, it seemed like everybody in the world knew my name. Whether I was licking an ice cream cone at Braum's or loading a cart with cans at Aldi, I heard someone whisper, "That's her! That's Jinger!" I felt strangely on display, like people knew something about me that I didn't.

My younger brothers and sisters frowned with confusion when strangers said hello to them. "How do they know my name, Mom?" they asked.

Mom smiled. "Well, they watch our lives on TV," she explained.

Mom taught us to be gracious when we met fans of the show, even if they didn't quite know what to say. "Wow, you're a lot thinner than you look on TV!" I heard more than once. I laughed at that comment. They weren't wrong. I'd watched the show myself, and the saying that the camera adds ten pounds is all too true.

Fans of the show often asked to take pictures with me. "Do the thumbs-up!" someone inevitably said before the camera snapped. I gritted my teeth and smiled as I obliged them. I knew they were referring to our show's opening credit sequence. For some reason, I gave the camera a thumbs-up when they filmed my shot. I had no idea why, since it's not something I normally do. That one impulsive gesture became my accidental trademark.

As TLC ordered more seasons, I became known as the girl with a million expressions, apparently because of my exaggerated faces. People even called me the "rebel Duggar," which was funny considering I wanted nothing more than to please my parents. It was all because of one offhand comment I made on camera about how I love the city and enjoy visiting it. That innocent statement turned into entire Reddit threads about how I wanted to move away from my family and lead an exciting life in the big city. Even people I met when I was out and about mentioned it from time to time. *But I'm a teenager!* I thought incredulously. *I'm not going anywhere!*

I didn't let the falsehoods faze me. I knew in my heart what was true, and no one could change that. Instead, I learned to be careful. I learned to think before speaking, to consider how what I was about to say might look splashed across the cover of a grocery store tabloid. I learned to listen carefully to questions I was asked in interviews for the show and to think through how my answer could be twisted to play up drama. I learned I shouldn't roll my eyes or make a face when the cameras were around—though sometimes it was hard to resist. Once I knew people thought it was funny, I definitely played up my facial expressions on occasion.

Watching myself on TV was bizarre. I was in my awkward teenage years, and I cringed when I saw my hair frizzing in the Arkansas humidity or a shirt that looked less than flattering, even though I had changed my clothes three times before the cameras arrived that day. I liked to think of myself as mature beyond my years, and my cheeks burned when I heard myself say something that made me sound like a kid. *Oh, why did I say that?* I thought. I made up my mind to say as little as possible when the cameras were around. I thought the less I said, the more mature I looked. That made for even more awkward interviews.

I wanted to believe that my friends saw me the same way they always had. After all, I was the same person I'd been before the cameras entered my life. And yet, there was tension. Though no one said anything to my face, I knew some of their families thought it wasn't holy to be on TV, and that made me feel uncomfortable.

Mom listened sympathetically when I told her about another strained conversation with a friend. "Maybe they're jealous, Jinge," she said.

I looked up in surprise. How could these girls be jealous of me?

"Some of your friends live in families a lot like ours," Mom continued. "They might be wondering why you're on TV and they're not. Especially when being on TV means your family gets to take exciting trips and do exciting things just so the crew can film an episode. Put yourself in their shoes."

I nodded slowly. I knew she was right. Still, I couldn't change the fact that my family had a TV show. "But what do I do?" I asked.

"I try to avoid mentioning the show as much as I can." Mom looked into my eyes, her gentle voice serious. "It's not the focus of our lives. We don't need to include it in our conversations with friends."

"How do you do that? I mean, the cameras are at our house so much."

"Well, when somebody asks what I did yesterday, I tell them I went shopping or had coffee with Grandma Duggar," she said. "I don't mention that the crew was there too."

Mom gave me a hug and smiled. "Be a sweet friend. Even when it's hard."

I took Mom's words to heart. I knew they were wise and necessary. They were also much harder than I thought they would be. I found myself mentally editing my stories and leaving out major pieces of information as I tried not to make my friends feel less than or left out. Even exciting news, like whether my pregnant mom was having a boy or girl, had to be kept under wraps if it hadn't yet been shared on the show. Conversations with anyone outside my family left me feeling as if I were holding back, unable to fully be myself.

At the same time, I knew it wasn't easy to be my friend. Girls I invited over for a cookout in the backyard might be asked to step to the side so they weren't in a shot. I felt terrible as I watched them sit in folding chairs near the side of the room instead of on a sofa, trying to avoid the cameras. Sometimes I wanted to shout, "Can we please not film today?" I wouldn't have blamed them for finding an excuse not to accept my next invitation to come over, or slowly fading into the background of my life, but some stayed faithful. They stuck by me and my family even when it was difficult or painful, even when our circumstances kept us from being as close as we once had been.

It wasn't long before I learned there was another kind of friend entirely. The kind who was all too eager for an invitation to my house. The kind that asked, not so subtly, if the crew would be there when I asked them to come over, or even showed up uninvited when they knew we were filming. The kind that quoted something I said on the show as if she had been there. I wanted to trust everybody with open arms, but I couldn't help but eye these girls with suspicion. *Do you genuinely care about me?* I thought, looking at her face intently. *Do you really want to be my friend? Or is it all about the show?*

"Yes, these people might be here for the wrong reasons," Mom said when we vented our frustrations. "But we need to be loving anyway."

Mom and Dad were quite serious about showing love. They opened their arms to everyone, even the most rabid fans, at least in the beginning. Family after family wrote to us and sent us e-mails asking if they could visit. Many were families with a lot of kids who planned to travel in our direction and wanted to stop by for dinner or even to stay the night. Mom and Dad said yes as often as they could.

It wasn't that I minded giving up my bed to sleep on a couch or eating with strangers. Most of us kids enjoyed the company and thought it was exciting to meet someone new. My complaint was the dinner I knew we'd be served. Inevitably, when Mom checked with a visitor to find out what they liked to eat, they would say, "We aren't picky, but we'd love some of that tater tot casserole."

Mom had fixed us that meal for years, but since it was featured in our first documentary, it had become the Duggar family signature meal. As families streamed in and out of our house, I grew to the point of feeling sick looking at the concoction of tater tots, ground turkey, and cream of mushroom soup.

Most visits were sweet times of fellowship with Christian families.

We had a few odd visits here and there, like the family that complained our house smelled of bleach and immediately ran through the main floor opening all the windows. But nothing deterred Mom and Dad from opening our home to strangers—until the diary incident.

It was Fourth of July weekend, and several friends and family members had planned to visit, when a college student wrote asking if she could stop by. "I watch your show, and I'd love to come and meet your beautiful family," her e-mail said. Mom and Dad thought she sounded sweet, so they welcomed her in like they did most anyone else.

By now, we had an entire routine for when fans visited. Whether they were staying the night or for dinner, we almost always started with a tour of the house. All of us were prepared to herd tour groups to the girls' room, the boys' room, the laundry room, and the massive pantry. When the college girl visited that Fourth of July weekend, she accompanied one of my brothers as well as a few other visitors on a tour. No one questioned the backpack she wore, and she seemed nice enough. She left as the day wound to a close, and I didn't give the matter another thought. That is, until a month and a half later, when I heard Dad call my name over the house's intercom system.

"Jinger, can you come up to the office, please?" his voice echoed off the tile floors of the kitchen.

I climbed the stairs and found him sitting in front of his computer, a confused sort of half smile on his face.

"Hey, Jinge," he said, uncertain how to begin. "This is really funny. Maybe the funniest thing I've seen in a while. But, somebody's claiming to have your journal."

I stared at him in disbelief. What he said couldn't be possible. My diary was safely in my dresser where I always kept it. Wasn't it?

"One of my friends sent me this eBay listing." Dad grabbed his mouse and clicked on the Internet browser. "This looks like yours, doesn't it? Whoever has it is trying to sell it for $100,000."

A creepy feeling overwhelmed me as I leaned forward and squinted at the computer screen. There it was. I had no doubt that was my diary. *Are you kidding me?* I thought, feeling completely violated. *Who's been in my bedroom?*

The person who created the ad posted a picture not only of the cover, but also of a page I'd written inside. I was mortified. Not because of anything I'd written—when you have eighteen siblings, you learn pretty quick not to write anything deeply personal in a book a sibling could get their hands on. I was much more embarrassed by my terrible handwriting. Girls are supposed to have pretty, dainty cursive, with *i*'s dotted with hearts. My writing looked more like a ten-year-old boy's.

"This is crazy," Dad said. "We have to figure out who did this."

Word spreads fast in a family as big as ours. Dad and I were still in the office brainstorming who might be the culprit as the older kids overheard us and ran into the office.

We were stumped. We knew plenty of strangers had been in and out of our house. We tried to remember who might have acted shifty or wandered off by themselves at any point during a tour. No one had any leads.

"Where is this person from?" somebody shouted. "Who's the seller?"

The seller's name was unlisted, but the location wasn't. At first, the little Wisconsin town didn't ring any bells. Then, one of my brothers' eyes lit up.

"Wait, wait, wait," he said, quieting the rest of us down. "The only person I can think of from Wisconsin is that girl who visited back at the Fourth of July. What was her name?"

A quick search of Dad's e-mail revealed the girl's contact information. There in her address was the same little town from the eBay listing.

"That's her," we immediately said. "No one else could have done this."

Dad was completely calm as he e-mailed the college girl to say she needed to return the diary, or she'd be prosecuted. She responded right away, to my surprise.

"I'm sending it back," she said. "I didn't read it, don't worry." That statement wasn't overly comforting, given that she'd posted a picture of my open diary on the Internet.

True to her word, though, the diary arrived a few days later, along with a DVD. We watched in fascination as the DVD played a fifteen-minute recording of the girl apologizing to us. The whole incident was enough to convince my parents that maybe we needed to be more careful about who we allowed in our house.

Yet even when it would have been easy to become cynical, Mom and Dad pointed us back to Christ. Yes, these situations were unusual at best. But these were the trials that come with being blessed with a platform. Mom and Dad reminded us that our platform also brought us untold joy and opportunities to share the love of Christ. The stacks of fan mail we received also included letters from women in abusive relationships, kids without loving homes, people in situations I couldn't even fathom. Somehow, they saw our show and saw hope. They saw the light of Jesus shining in us and wanted what we had. People wrote to us to share that they gave their lives to Christ because they watched our show. Everywhere I went, I heard from someone whose life had been changed because of our impact.

In those moments, I knew that whatever discomfort I experienced was worth it. That my momentary problems were so minor in light of eternity. For reasons I still don't understand, God gave me and my family a voice to reach the masses. Our job was to guard ourselves from pride and stay faithful. It wasn't easy. But it was worth it.

Chapter Four

"Dreams Change"

Jeremy

Freezing cold air cut through the doors of the rental car as I drove through the streets of northern Finland. It was well past midnight when I landed in the Oulu airport after a long flight from Philadelphia, but I was too excited to feel tired yet. I knew Finland was a great place to begin my career as a professional soccer player.

Over the past couple of years, I'd strived to honor Christ as I led the FCA chapter I'd started. Although I was far from perfect, I'd experienced victory over sins that had become patterns in my life. I wanted to know Christ and keep the promise I'd made to serve Him with my life. I'd finished my degree, gotten an agent, and gone to the United Soccer League combine, where I competed against other standout players for a chance at the pros. I even got some interest from a couple of Major League Soccer teams, but they didn't want me as a starter. My eyes were fixed on the goal of playing professionally until I retired. Sitting on the bench wouldn't get me there. Instead, I signed a two-year contract to play soccer in Finland. It wasn't a top-tier league, but I'd be a starter, and I'd get some good experience under my belt.

In Finland, I woke up early each morning to get a head start on training, just like I had when I was a kid. It was always dark and freezing cold outside as I pulled on my hoodie and sweatpants before heading to the athletic center. Music blared from the speakers as I lifted weights, sprinted on the treadmill, and kicked the ball around. I was already warmed up and well into my workout when team training began for the day. Training for the first two months was grueling, unlike anything I'd ever experienced. But I knew that this was what it took to be the leader of the pack, to stand out, and to hopefully catch the attention of a bigger club.

My first year in Finland couldn't have gone better if I'd planned it. I signed for AC Oulu, a team in a small northern town with cobblestone roads and weekend meat markets. The team was coached by Juha Malinen, a passionate and energetic coach, and had some remarkably talented players. That season, I had eleven shutouts in twenty-four games, which attracted interest from the big leagues back in the US where I ultimately hoped to play. But even while I was living my dream, I felt a tension.

I can trace that tension back to my first Sunday at Oulu Christian Fellowship. When I arrived in Finland, I'd sought out a church home right away and somehow stumbled into this simple gathering of Christians in a university chapel. Before long, I found myself attending the church's Bible studies. That first week, I sat in a circle on the floor, my leather Bible in my lap, my eyes focused on a passage in the Gospel of Matthew.

"So, what does this passage mean to you?" the leader asked.

What does it mean to me? I didn't know what that meant. I didn't grow up asking questions like that about Scripture. God's Word is his authoritative self-revelation to the world. I had never thought to ask what it meant to me, but simply, what does it mean? Up until that point, I'd assumed that everyone understood it the same way I did. I was only twenty-two years old, certainly not the oldest or most mature person in the room, but I felt that I had to speak up.

"Well..." I said slowly, searching for the right words. "What does it actually say?"

I could feel the rest of the group staring at me. This wasn't the kind of question they were used to discussing.

I kept going. Without realizing what was happening, I was suddenly digging into the passage, explaining what it meant with an authority I didn't know I had.

As I kept attending Bible studies, other group members turned to me more frequently for explanations of a difficult passage or answers to theological questions. The church even asked me to speak one Sunday. As parishioners sought me out for counsel, I found myself in the trenches, side by side with church members. People invited me into the messy and difficult parts of their lives, knowing I would help them without judgment. It was exhilarating. I wanted to care for souls. I wanted to care for this church.

My laser focus was suddenly split. My mind drifted to the church as I lifted weights and trained. I could feel the pull toward ministry almost as if something was physically tugging at my body. Once, a friend even mentioned it to me.

"Jeremy, I think you've got the gift of discernment and teaching," he said.

I shrugged and thought to myself, *Maybe down the road, but I've got soccer.*

I wasn't completely ignoring God's call. I could see myself standing at a pulpit one day, counseling struggling parishioners, preaching the gospel. But I figured that was a long way off, after I retired from a long and lucrative soccer career. I saw ministry as a retirement job or a backup plan in case the whole soccer thing didn't work out.

I had finished my first year in Finland when my agent called with good news. The New York Red Bulls, one of the top clubs in the country, had seen me play, and they were interested. At first, I was nervous. I still had a year left on my contract with Finland, and anyone who signed me had to pay a transfer fee.

After speaking with the Red Bulls' team manager, I spent the next few days on pins and needles. He seemed interested in me, but I didn't want to get my hopes up only to have them dashed. The decision was out of my hands, beyond my control, and solely up to God.

I was visiting my parents in Pennsylvania a few days later when my agent called. I had finished the hardest part of my P90X yoga workout and had to catch my breath before answering. I pressed the phone up to my ear and listened closely, trying to block out the sound of the violin lesson my mom was teaching in the next room as I listened to my agent. He told me the New York Red Bulls were willing to pay the transfer fee. They wanted me. I was going to be an MLS goalkeeper. It had been my dream since I was twelve years old. The dream others had told me was impossible was coming true.

This call was the end of my waiting, the end of anxiously wondering if all my work would pay off, the end of crying out to God for peace in my mental turmoil. At the same time, a new chapter was beginning. I'd be on the field with players I admired on TV, players who were revered around the world. I'd be playing in one of the greatest cities in the world, a place I could explore and experience as a young single guy. Living in New York, I'd even be able to attend Tim Keller's famous church, Redeemer Presbyterian Church. One phone call and the whole trajectory of my life had changed. It felt surreal and thrilling all at once.

My dad knew what I was about to tell him before I could say a word. The news was barely out of my mouth as he embraced me in a hug. "Praise God!" he said over and over.

Mom was in the room as soon as her violin student closed the front door. Her eyes shimmered with tears as I told her I was going to be a Red Bull. She wrapped me in her arms as she had my whole life, as if I was still her little boy and not a grown man. Gratitude overwhelmed me.

• • •

I arrived in New York on a blustery, cold January day. The team paid for a town house outside the city in Secaucus, New Jersey, close to our training facility. It also happened to be near my grandparents. We'd already arranged to meet for dinner every week, which was an unexpected blessing of my new position.

Snow covered the ground around our outdoor training field, but our turf was cleared. All of us were bundled up in our warmest athletic gear as manager Hans Backe blew the whistle to begin practice. I was thankful we'd already had a meet and greet at Red Bull Arena. Otherwise, I might have had a hard time keeping my jaw off the ground as I jogged down the field with Thierry Henry, Rafa Márquez, and other soccer legends. I stifled a grin as Rafa scored a near-post header. *Rafa Márquez scored a goal on me!* I thought.

I definitely needed to level up. The speed of play was drastically faster than that of college teams or the league in Finland had ever been, and even as a goalkeeper, I had to step up to think ahead. As the preseason began, though, I felt good. I was playing well, I was bonding with the guys on the team, and I was enjoying myself.

When the Red Bulls brought me on, they also recruited another goalkeeper, Ryan, who I immediately liked. Both of us were solid goalkeepers, but we had very different styles. I was loud and vocal, while Ryan was more reserved. Neither style is better, they're just different. Slowly, I noticed the manager picked Ryan to play more preseason games than me, and if I got to play, Ryan always started the game. When the time came for our first regular season game, I wasn't surprised when the manager went with Ryan instead of me.

That's OK, I told myself. *I'll get my chance.*

In a normal season, that's probably how things would have played out. But Ryan had the kind of breakout season goalkeepers dream of. He went on a tear, with no slipups, no mistakes, and no reason for the manager to take him out. The entire league was talking about him. It was the kind of season I wanted my rookie year. Instead, I was sitting on the bench.

I didn't blame the manager. I knew he was under pressure to have the team perform well, and that the decisions he made were nothing personal. And I was happy for Ryan, I truly was. Still, as a competitor, it hurt.

Game after game I sat on the bench, and I began to realize that it was affecting my joy of the game. I didn't have the same sense of freedom anymore at practices. The magic of the smell of the grass, the tying of my cleats, the touch of the ball, was fading. I found myself trying to adapt styles, hoping that would be the key, that maybe the manager would notice.

Our team sports psychologist, Marc Sagal, listened and nodded as I poured out my heart to him during a session one day.

"Jeremy, you're not playing for the love of the game," he said. "You're playing for the manager's approval, not for the love of the game, aren't you?"

I nodded slowly. As Marc said the words out loud, it was clear to me. I wasn't playing for the love of the game and God's glory. I was playing for my manager's approval.

"My advice to you is, name it and tame it," Marc said. "The only way you're going to change how you feel is to recognize when you're feeling this way, and then deal with it."

"Name it and tame it," I repeated. Marc was exactly right. I couldn't control the thoughts that drifted into my head, but I could control what I did with them. I had to recognize when I had wrong thinking, understand what caused it, and shift my thoughts to truth. I had to stop changing who I was and worrying about the manager's perception.

My resolve was put to the test when Ryan was injured later that year. I thought for sure this was my chance. Instead, the team brought in someone else. *Are you kidding me?* I thought when I heard the news. *They're not even going to give me a shot?*

Eventually, the team brought on a new goalkeeper named Luis Robles. I knew from the first day we trained together that there was something I liked about this guy. Soon, I discovered what it was. He was a Christian too. The guy who should've been my rival quickly became one of my best friends and a mentor. We trained together and shared hotel rooms when the team traveled. It was on one of those trips that Luis shared a story about how the Lord humbled him, delivering him through his lowest moments and deepest heartbreaks before bringing him to the Red Bulls. As we sat in our room, I couldn't help but weep as Luis described the way God had shattered his pride. *This is exactly what's happening to me,* I thought.

"Your identity isn't in soccer," Luis told me. "That's why God broke down my pride. He was showing me that my identity has to be found in Christ."

As shaky as my career had become, my walk with the Lord was thriving. Since I'd moved to New York, I'd been involved in a small group from Redeemer that met at an apartment in Chelsea, about twenty blocks from Times Square. We studied the Word and went out for pizza that first week, and I found myself sitting next to the group leader, James Song. On paper, we were two very different people—he was a successful businessman, the son of Korean immigrants, and I was a white athlete. But we were both driven. We both loved Christ. And we both loved good food.

Our conversation over pizza blossomed into a close friendship. Whether we were drinking coffee or eating Korean barbecue, we rarely talked about work. We could spend hours talking about Scripture and theology. The more James and I got to know each other, the more he drew me into leadership. He encouraged me to teach and offer insights in our little Bible study. Before long, people came to us for counsel on spiritual doubts, struggling relationships, and battles with addictions. I felt just as I had back in Finland. Even though I hadn't gone out looking for the opportunity, I was ministering again, and it felt good.

Once again, though, the tension within me returned. There I was, playing with some world-class players. And, even if I wasn't playing, I was living the dream. But it wasn't fulfilling. The tension was getting stronger, louder.

And then, the mass exodus came. The entire coaching staff and seventeen players, including me, were sent packing in the off-season as the team cleaned house. *I'm only two years into my soccer career*, I thought. *This is my dream. Where will I end up next?*

When one of my Red Bull teammates Teemu Tainio told me he was going to be playing in Finland, I thought I might have my answer. It was an elite club known as HJK, and they invited me to come out for a two-week trial in Spain. I played well, got a shutout against Strømsgodset IF, a top club from Norway, and the whole team and staff seemed to like me. I came home thinking it was a sure thing.

Back in the States, I waited for a call. It wasn't the MLS, but I was excited to get back to playing, to get another chance. *When you sign with HJK, you really need to focus on your career and put ministry on the back burner*, I told myself. *Soccer is your priority. Not ministry.*

I was still in bed when I heard my phone vibrate. It was a text from my agent. I expected to read good news. "Unfortunately, Jeremy, HJK said no. I will call you later today. Sorry."

I sat the phone on the nightstand and closed my eyes, my head spinning. This wasn't what was supposed to happen. I felt crushed with disappointment, too discouraged to even get out of bed. *I can't deal with this right now*, I thought. I rolled over and went back to sleep.

"I don't know what to do," I wrote in my journal later that day. "I am struggling to pray, because I don't know what to say. I will ask for peace and guidance. I will praise Him. This is it. This is an occasion to be most satisfied in God in the midst of loss, anxiety, distress. God is a loving father who gives good gifts. He is ordaining everything for my good. Right now, I am deflated, uncertain, and sad."

Within a day or so, something shifted inside me. After months of pushing ministry to the back burner, my heart changed. I told my dad that if a club didn't call in the next two days, I would enroll in seminary.

Ironically, a North Carolina team called two days later. I took that as providence showing me God wanted me to keep playing soccer. But the two weeks of training felt like torture. Each day, I gritted my teeth and slogged through practice without an ounce of passion. I didn't want to be there. All I wanted to do was get back to my hotel room and study my Bible.

When team management told me they weren't going to offer me a contract, it was all I could do to stifle a smile. "No problem," I told them. "I'm going to seminary."

I was completely serious. My desire to play had evaporated. I was sure now that God wanted me in ministry, and He didn't want me to wait. I didn't understand how my lifelong dream had suddenly turned into a chore. When I told my friend Tomer Chencinski about it, though, he wasn't surprised.

"Dreams change," Tomer said. I was struck by how profound two simple words could be. I wasn't giving up on my old dream. God was giving me a new one instead. He was showing me ministry wasn't a backup plan at all. It wasn't a consolation prize. The gift of ministry was far greater than any soccer career could ever be. I wasn't begrudgingly accepting ministry. I wanted it. I opened my laptop to announce my retirement.

This is the part where my story takes a detour. I was serious when I wrote that blog post. I planned to enroll in an online seminary and start taking classes right away. Two days later, though, a second division San Antonio soccer team sent me a Facebook message. The goalkeeping coach had seen me play and wanted me to come train with his team. I told him no. I'd decided to pursue ministry. Why would I go back to soccer already? But the coach was persistent, and his offer was generous.

"Jeremy, you're what, twenty-five?" Luis asked when I told him the situation. "Just go do it. You're not turning your back on ministry. You have plenty of time."

So, I flew to San Antonio for five days of training. The goalkeeping coach encouraged me to embrace who I was, to play my heart out, and not worry about what anyone thought. With his blessing, I was back to my loud, vocal style and loving every minute of it. I also got connected with Grace Community Church of San Antonio and met the pastor, Tim Conway—a godly man who offered to let me live with him and his family if I played there. He promised to help mold and shape me as I prepared myself for ministry. San Antonio seemed like the best of both worlds. I had no reservations in saying yes when the head coach offered me a two-year contract.

I moved to San Antonio with very clear commitments. I wanted to know God more intimately, grow in my theological knowledge, and develop as a clear teacher. I wanted to grow in holiness.

For the next two years, I gave the team my all on the field. Off the field, Pastor Tim mentored me, helping me grow in my faith. At church and in Bible study, I surrounded myself with godly men who astounded me with their deep knowledge of God's Word. I realized how green and naive I really was, and how much I had to learn. Even as I discovered my inadequacy, my desire for ministry took off. I was up by 5:15 each morning, not to train anymore, but to study the Bible, to pray, to memorize Scripture. Spending time with God wasn't an obligation. Just as soccer once had an irresistible pull, now all I wanted to do was dive into the Scriptures.

While I was committed to playing soccer and fulfilling my contract, I sought out every ministry opportunity I could. I started a Bible study for anyone who wanted to learn more about God, right in our team locker room after training. All I did was order a pizza and share the gospel. And to my surprise, week after week guys actually showed up. Some of them openly admitted they didn't believe the gospel, and yet they kept coming back.

Even as soccer once again became more of a chore, I was excited to be in San Antonio. It felt like I was in an intensive ministry program, and I was seeing the benefits. I was growing, both in knowledge and in wisdom. I was teaching, whether it was a youth group or a Bible study at church. But I still thought leading a church was years down the road. The more I grew, the more I realized how much growth I still needed.

Then, Pastor Tim called me and a good friend, Zeek Coleman, into his office. I had no idea what was coming when he sat us down and told us about a church plant in Laredo that had lost its pastor. He needed someone to oversee the work and make sure the small congregation flourished.

"I'd like you two to do it," he said.

I was floored. Sure, I wanted ministry, but I didn't think it would happen so quickly. I'd spent the last two years learning how inadequate I was and now I was supposed to oversee a church?

I told the pastor I'd pray about it. As I sought the Lord, I felt an overwhelming peace. I knew I had to do this. I wasn't ready. I wasn't good enough. But if God was directing me to enter ministry, His grace would be sufficient. I was exhilarated and terrified all at once as I said yes.

Chapter Five

Different

Jinger

If you had asked one of my brothers or sisters if I was a Christian, they would have said yes without hesitation. No one doubted I was a believer. I didn't either—at first.

I was young, maybe five years old, when I prayed the prayer of salvation with Mom and Dad. Jessa had just run excitedly into the girls' room to tell me she'd prayed with Mom and Dad, and that she was a Christian now. She and I were the best of friends, and anything she did, I wanted to do too. *I want to be a Christian too!* I remember thinking. That same night, I asked my parents to pray with me too, and they did so gladly.

I have no doubt that children can come to know the Lord at a young age. The Lord invites the children to come to Him, and many do. But for me, looking back, it's clear I mainly wanted to be like my big sister and do what she did. I didn't genuinely understand my need for a savior. This became apparent as the days went on—there was no fruit of true conversion in my life. Praying that prayer didn't change me. I was the same Jinger I had always been.

On the outside, I did all the right things. I knew the right answers in church, I joined in service projects without complaining, and I memorized

Scripture with the rest of the family. I was sweet to the people around me and avoided getting into trouble. I even got baptized. But none of it was the result of the Holy Spirit working inside me. I naturally had an easygoing temperament, and I didn't like to rock the boat. I wasn't really trying to glorify God through my actions. It was all for me. I wanted to be liked. I wanted everyone to think well of me and praise me, so I did what was expected of me.

One morning when I was about twelve, I woke up early, before anyone's alarm went off or the first cup of coffee was poured. I tiptoed through the house, trying to make as little noise as possible as I bleached the bathrooms, wiped down counters, and picked up stray toys or schoolbooks left out the night before. By the time the sun streamed through the big front windows, the floors were spotless, and the house was neat and clean.

Mom rubbed the sleep from her eyes as she came down the stairs and gasped. "Jinger!" she exclaimed when she saw me in the living room, looking pleased with myself. "Did you do all this?"

I basked in Mom's praise, taking in every "ooo" and "ahh" as she gushed over my handiwork. "You did such a good job, Jinge! This is so amazing!"

Her praise felt so good that I wanted more. So, after a while, I did it again. Everyone assumed I was being selfless, that I loved to serve, and that I had a heart for helping others. While those were certainly factors, they weren't my only motivation. I wanted approval. Mom's words validated what I longed to believe about myself. If Mom said I was good, it must be true.

As I grew older, I noticed little hints here and there that I wasn't like everybody else in my family. From the time we were tiny, we were taught to read our Bibles and pray every day. This wasn't meant to be an item on our to-do list, but we were told it was the best way to grow closer to the

Lord and abide in Christ. But to me, reading my Bible felt no different than any of the "jurisdictions"—my chores I was responsible for. I definitely didn't do it every day, and when I did, I barely opened my Bible for five minutes. I read the words without letting them penetrate my heart. I never put down my Bible feeling inspired or motivated to serve the Lord. I was mostly relieved to have the job done.

Jessa, however, loved to study God's Word. Almost every day, I'd find her sitting cross-legged on her bed with her Bible on her lap, absolutely engrossed in Scripture. She didn't only want to read a chapter or two. She wanted to dig into each verse, to get to the bottom of what God was really saying. She was convicted, challenged, spurred to action. I listened to her chatter about the armor of God or a verse in Philippians and felt suddenly out of place. All our lives, Jessa and I had everything in common. Now, there was a disconnect. *I don't have the desire for that*, I thought. *I wish I did. But I don't.*

All around me, I saw examples of true devotion to the Lord, not just in my siblings but in Mom, Dad, and especially Grandma Duggar. No matter the struggle or difficulty, she always told me that God is faithful. I grew up hearing her tell the story that all started with a jar of rice. Back when Dad was a kid, Grandma Duggar used to keep a mason jar of rice on her dining room table as a decoration. Their family was in a season of financial struggle when one morning they opened the pantry and discovered there was nothing to eat for breakfast. "Well, we have this jar of rice," Grandma Duggar said, soothing her children.

She turned that decoration into a filling breakfast and said, "We just need to pray that God will provide for us." That very day, a bag of groceries showed up on their doorstep. Every Thanksgiving, when we went around the table and shared what we were thankful for, we knew what Grandma Duggar was going to say before she opened her mouth. "God's faithfulness," she said each time. "He's always so faithful to me." I admired her faith and wished I felt the same way. But I didn't.

Each Sunday I sat quietly in the pew, hearing the sermon but not truly listening. It was all I could do not to look at the clock as my stomach growled. *Is he really going to preach for forty-five minutes?* I'd think. I was much more interested in the potluck after the service and the chance to talk to my friends than anything the pastor had to say.

I was twelve when I began waking in the middle of the night. Sometimes it was because of a bad dream or a thunderstorm, which were common in Arkansas in the springtime. Other times, my eyes snapped open in the dark for no reason at all. I squeezed my eyes shut, trying to will myself back to sleep. Instead, my mind swirled in an endless spiral of fear. *What if there's a tornado? What if Mom or Dad get cancer? What if I get cancer? What if I get in a car accident?*

The fears usually culminated with one terrifying, all-consuming question: *If I died tonight, would I go to heaven?* My brain told me the answer was yes. We'd been taught that if we ever questioned whether we were saved, we could look back on that day we prayed the prayer of salvation and feel confident. But I know now that salvation doesn't come simply by muttering words in a prayer, and it certainly isn't just a feeling. Salvation is the amazing transformation that happens when God changes someone from the inside out. Jesus called it the new birth. But at the time, all I felt was fear. Was I trusting in Jesus' work on the cross or in my own good deeds? Was I saved? More and more, the sinking feeling in my heart told me I wasn't. I lay in bed night after night, gripped with fear, too afraid to let myself drift back to sleep. Sometimes I tried to pray, but it felt pointless. I wasn't right with God. Why would he listen?

Mom had always told us that any time any of us needed to talk, we could wake her, no matter how late it was. That's a powerful statement from a woman with nineteen children, and she meant it. I took her up on that offer more nights than I could count. I practically wore a path from the girls' room to Mom and Dad's during this period of fear.

"Mom," I'd whisper as she opened her eyes. "I can't sleep. I have so much fear."

Mom never told me to go back to bed or sighed with frustration when I appeared at the side of her bed. I was never an inconvenience. She sat with me for hours in her room, listening patiently as I poured out my fear that I wasn't saved. She quoted Scriptures, especially Romans 10:13—"For whosoever shall call upon the name of the Lord shall be saved" (KJV). She prayed with me and only sent me back to bed when I was ready.

But the fears didn't stop. My nighttime awakenings became so frequent that Dad wrote out Scriptures about fear and worry for me on a sheet of spiral notebook paper. I read them dutifully and convinced myself I wasn't afraid anymore. In the blackness of night, though, I forgot every verse I'd read.

During the day, fears endlessly scrolled through my mind. I worried constantly about whether people liked me, or what they thought of me, or if that thing I'd said sounded stupid. I felt a constant drive to be perfect. The perfect daughter. The perfect sister. The perfect friend. The perfect Christian. I wanted Mom and Dad to think well of me, and one mistake was enough to devastate me. *Oh, I failed! I failed!* I thought over and over.

I told myself my thoughts were normal. I was a people pleaser. All teenagers worry about what other people think. I didn't want to admit that selfishness was taking root in my heart. Every desire to please others and make a good impression all came down to me, me, me. It wasn't satisfying. It was exhausting.

One fear, the most insidious of all, was also the most pervasive. Each morning as I fixed my hair and adjusted my skirt in the mirror, I frowned at the girl staring back at me. I was going through the awkward phase that everyone experiences in their adolescence. The changes I saw in my body were normal and natural. To me, though, they were unacceptable. I hated the way I looked. I was convinced I was fat and getting fatter by the day.

I'm so ugly, I scolded my reflection. *I need to do something about this. I need to be skinny.*

I know now, of course, that this was a lie from the enemy. Whatever I saw in the mirror was a complete distortion of reality. I couldn't see myself the way everybody else did.

One night, I weighed myself and noticed I'd gained half a pound. I panicked. Sure, I told myself, it's only half a pound now, but tomorrow it's a whole pound, then five, then ten, then more. *I have to do something*, I thought.

I didn't want to draw attention to my weight-loss efforts. If I turned down dinner, someone was sure to notice. Instead, I devised a plan. I decided the key to losing weight was eating fewer meals. The trick, however, was finding a way to do it without anyone noticing.

I skipped breakfast each morning by sleeping as late as I could, so that nobody would know I hadn't eaten. Then, I'd eat a super-light lunch and a healthy snack before dinner, so I could honestly say I wasn't hungry and pick at my food. At night, I'd go to bed before my stomach could rumble too loudly.

It seemed reasonable at the time. I didn't realize that my little weight-loss plan was teetering dangerously on the edge of an eating disorder.

I spent weeks pretending I wasn't hungry, ignoring the gnawing emptiness in my stomach. I went to bed when the hunger became too much. In the morning I'd stare at my reflection again, my eyes fixated on my imagined rolls of fat and nonexistent chubby cheeks. I walked away resolved to try harder. I had to be skinny. If this is what it took, then I would do it, I decided, no matter how hard it was.

Eventually I decided dairy must be the problem. Maybe all the cheese and milk in our house was making me fat. I swore off dairy of any kind, and if somebody asked about it, I had a response ready. "You know what, I think I'm allergic to dairy," I said. "I'm going to stay away from it for a while and see if I feel a little better."

When I stepped on the scale, I saw that my plan was working. I was losing weight. Yet I still wasn't satisfied. *Why can't I be skinny like the girls at church?* I thought desperately, hating my reflection in the mirror. *Maybe that's why no one likes me. Maybe if I were skinny, everybody would like me.* Looking back, it's clear this, too, was a lie. I had friends, dear friends! We loved spending time together. But the lies about my weight began affecting my view of my friends as well.

After a month of extreme dieting, I told my mom what was going on. I'm not sure what made me do it. Maybe even as a preteen, I could sense that my thoughts weren't healthy. Maybe I was afraid of the path I was on, especially since I knew my mom's history. Back when she was a teenager, Mom had battled with bulimia. We grew up hearing about her struggle with poor body image and an unhealthy relationship with food. I knew if anyone would understand what I was going through, it was Mom. I wasn't afraid of how she would react. I knew she would help, and deep down, I understood that I needed it.

If Mom was upset when I told her, she didn't show it. She didn't lecture me or insist that I eat fatty foods. She didn't cry out, "How can you think that!" when I told her that I thought I was fat and ugly. She was completely calm and compassionate as she said, "Thank you so much for telling me, Jinge." That's what she always said when I told her something difficult, even when I walked in expecting the hardest conversation in the world. It's something I still appreciate about her.

"It's great that you want to be healthy," she said. "Avoiding junk food and not overeating are good things. But you need to eat enough calories to fuel your body."

I nodded and sniffled, tears already rolling down my face. I usually ended up crying during our heart-to-heart conversations at some point or another.

"But all my friends are way skinnier than me!" I said. "I feel so fat when I'm around them, and I wish I could look like they do." My cheeks flushed as I pictured how thick my waist felt next to their slim bodies, how I could practically feel myself getting fatter with every bite of food I took.

Mom took a deep breath before she spoke. I know now she was probably collecting herself, pushing away the heartache of hearing her own daughter tear herself down.

"You are not them," she said firmly. "You can't try to be like anybody else. Your body is exactly as God made it to be. You need to see yourself as who you are in Christ."

Those words should have pierced my soul. All my life, I'd been told I was created in God's image, that my identity was found in Christ and not in my appearance. I knew it was true. But I didn't feel it. I looked down, not wanting Mom to see what I was thinking.

"How about I help you?" she offered. "We'll come up with a plan for you to be healthy. We'll do it together, you and me."

Mom's plan basically flipped my mindset from one that focused on being skinny to one that focused on health. She brainstormed healthy snacks and meals for me and never once insisted that I eat hot dogs or macaroni and cheese with everyone else. Her only requirement was that I eat about two thousand calories a day, enough for a healthy, growing girl.

Throughout the day, as I ate, I'd either let her know what I ate or send her a quick text. That way, she knew I was eating, and I knew someone would find out if I slipped back into my old habits.

The plan helped. I ate three healthy meals a day and snacked when I was hungry. I knew my mom was walking right alongside me, and that reassurance kept me on track. Inside, though, the wrestling continued. Those unhealthy thought patterns didn't disappear overnight. Sometimes, I found myself feeling uncomfortable as I stood among a group of friends, hoping my T-shirt and skirt disguised my figure.

I could feel myself beginning to crumble. The body image struggles, the consuming fears, the constant wrestling with God—it was too much. I was sick of putting on a show for everyone, pretending I was fine when in reality, I was broken. One day, when I was fourteen years old, I realized that the thought of going to bed that night only to wake up gripped in fear was too much. I couldn't do it anymore.

The house was hustling and bustling with activity as usual when I whispered to Mom, "Can we talk?"

Mom could tell from my face that it was serious. "Let's go find a quiet room," she said. This was easier said than done, even in a house as big as ours. The girls' room and boys' room are almost always occupied, and usually somebody was doing homework in Mom and Dad's room. Our go-to spot for quiet conversations was a storage room we called the prayer closet. Anyone could use it for prayer or a moment alone. There was even a little desk and chair where you could sit down.

We stepped inside, careful not to knock our heads on the slanted ceiling of the tiny room. I sank onto the carpet as Mom closed the door. I sat silently for a moment, waiting for the right words to come to me.

"OK Jinge, just tell me," Mom said, her eyes filled with concern. "What is it?"

Before I could speak a word, I burst into tears. Mom wrapped me in a hug as I wept. "Oh Jinge," she said as she rubbed my back to console me. Mom has always been the best listener. She never pushes me to talk but waits until I'm ready.

"I know I'm not saved, Mom," I finally stammered. "I know I prayed the prayer when I was little, but my heart is not right."

In an instant, I saw my sin for what it was. I thought of the moments when I worried about what people thought, the moments I said and did the right thing to make someone like me, the moments I'd read my Bible just long enough to say I'd done it. My so-called normal worries revealed themselves as selfishness as I sat on the Berber carpet. To the outside world, I led a moral, upstanding life, but that day, the Lord opened my eyes to how ugly and filthy my sin was. Tears poured from my eyes as I felt the weight of who I was and what I'd done.

Mom walked me through some of the same Scripture she'd shared with me those nights I came to her room in fear. This time, something clicked for me. The words, "whosoever shall call upon the name of the Lord shall be saved," were now filled with hope. I wasn't stuck like this, I realized. I wasn't doomed to spend the rest of my life waking up in the middle of the night in terror. There was hope. The Lord would rescue me from my sin, if I only turned to Him.

"Do you want to pray?" Mom asked. "How about I pray first, then you go?"

There was no sinner's prayer, no simple formula of words. I poured out my heart on the closet floor, crying out to the Lord and asking Him to save me. I don't know what I prayed or how I said it. What I remember most is the change I felt.

From the moment I opened that closet door, it was like I flipped a switch. I was drawn to the Bible and read each word voraciously. I couldn't get enough. Each passage I had once taken for granted was now vivid and alive. Now, instead of shutting the Bible and walking away without giving it a second thought, I was spurred to action. Prayer was no longer simply a sentence I muttered. It was my lifeline. I couldn't wait to spend time with the Lord and prayed throughout the day, not only when I was alone in my room.

I was so amazed by what the Lord had done for me that I wanted it for everyone else too. I thought of family members and friends who didn't know the Lord, people who might feel the same fear and hopelessness I once did. My heart broke for them and I was driven by a genuine desire for everyone to know Christ. I wrote letters to family members, sharing the gospel with them, and wherever I went, I carried gospel tracts in my purse in case the right opportunity came up. I was a little zealous at the time, but the desire in my heart was for people to find the same hope I had found.

My struggles with eating didn't disappear. Sometimes, even with Mom's help and with my heart grounded in Scripture, I felt myself slip back into my old thought patterns. I talked myself out of going to a girls' retreat because I worried they wouldn't serve healthy food there. I sometimes fasted for a day, not just because it enhanced my prayer life, but also because it could help me lose weight. When these things happened, Mom was still there walking with me, keeping me accountable. We prayed together, and slowly, I learned to see myself through the eyes of Christ.

I no longer lay awake at night worried about tornadoes, sickness, or death like I used to. Following Christ didn't take away my problems or erase my struggles, but now I wasn't paralyzed by them. The hope of Christ cast a new light on whatever darkness I encountered. Walking with the Lord made my fears seem smaller and more manageable. I wasn't a slave to them anymore. I could rest assured in the arms of my savior.

Chapter Six

Lonely in Laredo

Jeremy

Every last ounce of energy left my body as I collapsed on my couch. It was a Sunday night, and as usual, I was completely spent after a day of preaching and teaching. I'd run on pure adrenaline since the ten o'clock Bible study at Grace Community Church in Laredo. After that, I'd had a few minutes to glance over my sermon before preaching the morning service. After a potluck lunch at the church, I had led a group over to the local homeless shelter to give food to its residents and share the gospel with them. Then, I had a two-and-a-half-hour drive back to San Antonio, since I was living there and commuting to Laredo on the weekends.

By the time I pulled in the driveway of the house I shared with three other guys, I had nothing left. I spent my entire week gearing up for Sundays. They were the culmination of all my study and preparation. When they were over, I was always ready to crash and spend the rest of the day like a bum.

Most pastors I've spoken to feel this way. It's the same feeling I had after playing a soccer game—total exhaustion. The emotional, physical, spiritual, and mental output left me drained. But as always, within minutes of hitting the couch, the dark cloud of loneliness descended, at times so thick I could nearly cut it with scissors. I felt a massive lull drop over me. Here I was, with a day full of stories to tell, and no one to tell them to. I had no one to confide in, no one to talk to, no one's company to enjoy. My roommates came through the room every once in a while, but it wasn't the same. I didn't want a roommate. I wanted a wife.

I was the only single pastor I knew when I agreed to oversee the Laredo church as a volunteer pastor, along with my friend Zeek. And I was lonely. Don't get me wrong, I didn't spend my days moping and complaining about not being married. Life as a pastor was exhilarating.

Grace Community Church was a small congregation that met in a stonework house turned office building, the kind of place you might find a dentist's office or other small business. The main service was held in a stark white room with turquoise trim. It wasn't in the best part of Laredo, and its appearance certainly did nothing to attract people. One guy told me the first time he drove by the church, he thought it was a crack house.

Laredo is right on the border between Texas and Mexico, and if you didn't know better, you'd think you weren't in the United States. A majority of people there are Spanish-speaking Latinos, except for border patrol officers and their families. Although Laredo is very safe, just across the border is Nuevo Laredo, a battleground for Mexican drug cartels.

Zeek moved to Laredo with his wife and four children when we agreed to oversee the church, while I stayed in San Antonio and worked for another pastor's rental property business. He'd let me crash at his house on the weekends so I could be in town for Sunday services. I liked to walk the tree-lined streets when I stayed with him, listening to the cacophony of birds chirping and singing around me as I prayed and meditated on the Word. I always had to keep an eye out for stray dogs. I have more stories than I can count about throwing rocks to scare away huge angry dogs, helping to protect women and children from strays, and even being chased over a fence.

Right away, I began preaching every week and leading Wednesday night prayer meetings, driving to Laredo every Wednesday and Saturday. I counseled parishioners, taught Bible studies, and did everything a full-fledged pastor did. On paper, I wasn't prepared at all, yet I felt an incredible peace. The Lord led me to a place of weakness, where I had no choice but to depend on Him. I didn't have a lifetime of preparation and planning to rely on like I'd had as a soccer player. But God gave grace, and I was amazed at how sufficient that was.

While I hadn't attended seminary, my conversations with my dad in those days were like a master class in sermon preparation. Each week, he helped me outline my sermon from the text, and he looked over every sermon manuscript. After I preached, he watched the recording online and gave me feedback. It was a formative time in my growth as a preacher.

I was only in my late twenties when I arrived in Laredo, and I had the baby face that came with my youth. When I told people I was a pastor, more than a few asked, "You mean a youth pastor?" Once, when eating lunch with a church member at Rudy's BBQ, a man who stopped by our table laughed outright when I was introduced as my friend's pastor. He thought the introduction was a joke. When he realized that I actually was the pastor, I could tell he was a bit embarrassed. Several people commented that Laredo was a great stepping-stone, a place for me to cut my teeth on pastoral work before I moved on to bigger and better things. I didn't see it that way. I believed the Lord had led me there, and I thought I would stay there until either I died or the Lord made it abundantly clear that he wanted me somewhere else.

I meant it too. Yes, it was a small church with a living room–size sanctuary, but the work was exciting. God was moving in that church, and I couldn't get enough. I wanted to be around more often. I didn't like living in San Antonio and commuting. I felt like I was missing out, even though I was only a volunteer pastor. I didn't want this to be a part-time gig. I wanted to commit full time.

It wasn't until Sunday nights and Mondays, my days off, that loneliness sank in. I confided in fellow pastors about my struggle and my desire for a wife. They told me this season wouldn't last long. Some attempted to console me: "Jeremy, charm is deceptive, and beauty is fleeting." *Easy for you to say*, I thought. *You've got a gorgeous wife and two kids!*

"Your problem is you're too picky," I was often told. But I knew I wasn't. I just hadn't met my wife yet.

Since I had gotten serious about the Lord back in college, I hadn't dated much. I didn't want to get in a relationship unless I could see myself marrying the woman. Laredo wasn't exactly a hotbed of Christian singles, and while there were a few godly women at my church, I didn't feel it was appropriate to pursue someone at the church given my leadership position.

One woman back in San Antonio believed God had shown her I was going to marry her daughter, and it turned out her daughter believed this as well. The woman told me this on multiple occasions, even though I told her from the get-go that I wasn't interested. There wasn't anything wrong with this girl—she was a wonderful person who was a good friend, but there was no chemistry.

At one point, however, in a particularly heavy season of loneliness, I began to wonder if she was the one for me. I was alone in ministry and tired. *If I married her, I'd have a companion*, I thought. I prayed desperately, asking the Lord to make it clear whether I should pursue her or not. *Lord, by the end of this weekend, please give me some direction on this! Is she the one for me or not?* I prayed.

The next day, on the phone with my parents, I mentioned my struggle to my mom. I told her I'd asked God for clarity, and I heard a pause.

"Jeremy," she said, "don't doubt in the dark what God has shown you in the light."

She was right. Although she was an incredible girl, I knew she wasn't the one for me. Why would I allow my loneliness to convince me to marry someone who wasn't right for me?

"I would not give you our blessing to pursue her," Mom said.

"You have no idea what a relief that is," I told her.

I was willing to wait for the right woman. I knew from Scripture what a blessing a godly wife is.

It wasn't long after that when I had a conversation with a friend who was trying to understand what kind of woman I was waiting for.

"I want someone who's passionate about Christ," I told him. "Someone who will follow the Lord wherever He leads us. Someone with a servant's heart." I paused, then admitted, "And who I find attractive, too."

My friend burst out laughing before joking, "Jeremy, how old do you expect her to be? No one your age is like that!"

I smiled. I didn't think what I was looking for was far-fetched. "You know what? I'm going to write it down, because these are God-honoring qualities. I want a woman who loves Christ."

The next morning, I wrote exactly what I was looking for in my journal.

Monday, March 1, 8:50 a.m.

Lord, bring me a partner, please. One who is in love with Christ, with a visible passion, humble, meek, willing to forsake all to follow wherever You lead us. Not consumed with money and comfort. A wartime mentality. A servant, strong in faith. Walks consistently by faith. Lover of children. Physically attractive to me. Disciplined.

Healthy lifestyle. Acquainted with the type of Christianity I'm striving to live.

I shut my journal and didn't think much of the list I'd written as I went about my day.

• • •

About a week later, my phone vibrated in my pocket. It was a Sunday night, and I was helping a homeless man named Bobby take refuge at a San Antonio shelter. I glanced at my phone and read the text on the screen. "Guess who's at your house," a friend wrote.

It wasn't unusual for people to be at my house on Sunday nights. Nearly every week, I came home to a house full of people, mostly singles from the church in San Antonio who hung out and played Ping-Pong. There were often pizza boxes opened buffet-style in the kitchen. Usually, I met new people when I walked into my house.

"Who is it?" I texted back.

The response came back almost immediately. "Ben and Jessa Seewald."

I knew who that was without having to google them. Back when I'd lived with the pastor in San Antonio, he and his daughters watched *19 Kids and Counting*. I teased them about the show, and once, when I saw Ben and Jessa's wedding picture on the cover of *People* magazine, I took a picture of it and texted it to the family as a joke.

"No way, that's crazy!" I texted.

"You better hurry up and get home before they leave," my friend texted.

I wasn't about to leave Bobby before he was settled in, and if I missed Ben and Jessa, then so be it. I wouldn't be upset or anything. By the time

I got home a couple hours later, I figured there was no way they were still there.

I was wrong. The get-together was still going strong, with at least fifteen people in the house. I recognized Ben wearing a backward red hat and chatting by the couch with one of my friends, and there was Jessa nearby, with her trademark skirt and long brown hair. I introduced myself to Ben.

"Hey man, what's going on?" I said. "I'm Jeremy."

"Oh, hi!" Ben said, his voice warm and friendly. "I'm Ben. That's my wife Jessa over there." He pointed as Jessa looked at us and smiled.

"So, do people come over every week?" Ben asked.

"Pretty much. There are usually people here when I get home from Laredo. I pastor a church out there." I paused for a breath when Ben interrupted me.

"Um, do you have a bathroom?" he asked.

I must be boring this guy to tears, I thought. "Yeah, it's right over there." I pointed down the hall and watched Ben make what I thought was his desperate getaway from a dull conversation with me. *I guess that's the end of that*, I thought.

But it wasn't long before Ben rejoined me. "Sorry about that, man," he said. "Now tell me about this church in Laredo."

It turned out Ben and I had a lot in common. He was interested in ministry too, and it wasn't long before we were talking about one of my favorite subjects, theology. He also told me the wild story of how he and Jessa ended up at my house that night. They were in town and had planned to meet up with a friend named Matt, who Ben knew only through Facebook. Matt said he'd be at a fellowship that night and sent someone to pick them up at the River Walk in downtown San Antonio. Ben, who's the most trusting cat you'll ever meet, saw no problem with getting into a car with someone he didn't know and going to a stranger's house. The fellowship ended up being the gathering at my house, and Matt didn't even show up, but Ben and Jessa were having such a good time they decided to stay.

"Why don't you give me your number?" Ben said toward the end of the night. "We should stay in touch."

I gave him my number and even drove him and Jessa to the airport later that night, where they picked up their rental car. I figured we might text here or there.

I'm not sure who texted first, but soon we were chopping it up on a pretty regular basis about life, ministry, and random subjects. He would text as he listened to sermons and we hashed out the meanings of a text or a spiritual issue. Ben loved getting in the weeds of theology as much as I did. He was a young man, he loved the Lord, and I enjoyed our conversations. We opened up to each other pretty much right off the bat about our personal struggles and battles too. I've never been shy about getting vulnerable. I've always been an open book. A few weeks went by and I'd already come to think of him as a buddy.

"Hey bro, how can I be praying for you?" I texted him one Tuesday night.

He sent a prayer request and asked how he could be praying for me. I thought for a moment before my thumbs flew around the screen.

"Man, ministry is really hard when you're single," I responded. "I'm lonely. I'm pouring myself out to others but can get pretty lonely. Just pray that the Lord provides a wife." I'm not the kind of guy who gives a generic request when someone asks how they can pray for me. This was my reality, my daily struggle.

My phone vibrated and I glanced at the screen. "I know a few godly girls if you need any ideas," Ben texted with a wink face emoji.

I laughed to myself for a moment. Maybe it was a joke. Ben married into the biggest family I'd ever heard of, so I figured he must be talking about his sisters-in-law. I shoved my phone in my pocket without responding.

But I didn't forget about what Ben said. Was he serious? Did he know someone he thought was a good match for me? I couldn't get the thought out of my head. Ben was a great Christian guy with a good head on his shoulders. I hadn't met anybody I considered pursuing. If Ben said he knew some girls, maybe I should pay attention.

A few days later, I brought it up again. "So, when you said you knew some godly girls, were you serious about that?" I said. "What did you mean?"

I grabbed my phone a little faster than usual when I felt it vibrate with his response.

"Yeah, I know of a few," he said. "For example, my sisters-in-law are the best girls I know, and they've got friends that are pretty great as well."

I stared at the screen for a moment, not sure what to think. Ben knew me by now. He knew I was committed to Christ, and that I wanted a wife who felt the same way. He wouldn't recommend a woman to me unless she was serious about the Lord.

Ben's text kept going. "I'm not big on setting people up, because I know most people don't like to be set up, but I will be honest, and if I know of a godly girl, I'll suggest her to a godly guy."

I could tell he was serious. This was no flippant, offhand comment, and I couldn't bring myself to ignore it. I didn't know much about the Duggars except for glimpses here and there when the pastor's family watched it. I never pictured myself marrying a reality star. But I was open-minded.

Ben said instead of setting me up with someone, the best thing for me to do would be to get to know the entire family and let it happen naturally. It turned out the Duggars attended a conference in Texas every spring. Ben invited me to drive six hours to the conference, hang out with the family, and see what happened.

It sounds crazy when I tell the story. I'd only met Ben once and texted with him for a few weeks. Now I was supposed to jump in my car, go to this conference I'd never heard of, and hang out with a family I'd never met on the off chance that one of the daughters might like me? But somehow, it didn't sound crazy to me at the time. What if I really did meet someone? I was tired of being lonely. I sure wasn't meeting anybody doing what I was already doing. Worst case scenario, I'd go home with a story to tell.

So, I responded, "OK, cool." I was in.

• • •

Four weeks later, I pulled into the campus where the conference was being held. I'd spent the last five and a half hours driving up I-35 North, trying to imagine what the next few days would be like. I found the people Ben had said to look for and made my way to the campground, where most conference attendees parked their RVs and giant buses. Somebody pointed me in the direction of the Duggar bus, and the next thing I knew, I saw Ben and Jessa with a huge group I recognized as the Duggar family.

I shook hands with person after person as Jessa introduced me to the whole group. *Wow, I've never heard so many J names in one place!* I thought. It was surreal. One of the siblings handed me a burger hot off the grill and I sat in a camping chair as a few of Jessa's brothers engaged me in conversation.

If I expected love at first sight, I didn't get it. My interactions with the Duggar sisters were minimal. *They must really keep to themselves*, I thought. I'd find out later that men are a dime a dozen around the Duggar family. Since the day their first show aired, men across the country have mailed letters and even visited in person, hoping for a chance to marry one of them. The Duggar women probably looked at me and thought, "Dude, get in line."

I attended a few conference sessions but spent most of the week hanging out with Ben and Jessa. I knew I had quite a bit in common with them before I went to the conference, but I didn't realize how much we'd enjoy spending time together. Jessa loved to debate theology, and the three of us stayed up late into the night locked in what might look like an argument to an outsider. To us, it was a good time. By the end of the conference, I considered them close friends.

I didn't get much of a chance to connect with Jessa's sisters. As I drove home, though, one moment stuck out in my mind. Saturday night, at a party with another family, I'd noticed a girl who told me her name was Jinger. She wore a green dress that brought out her eyes, and when she smiled, her whole face lit up with the kind of beauty I hadn't seen often. *She's really cute*, I thought. There was no magic right off the bat, no instant spark. Still, I couldn't help thinking about it.

We'll see. Who knows? I thought as I drove away. *Maybe I'll visit them again one day.*

Chapter Seven

The Guy in the Sweater

Jinger

"Ben and I met the most awesome guy in San Antonio."

Jessa and I stood together, gazing out the kitchen window in the little house she shared with her new husband, Ben Seewald. I turned from the view of the front yard and looked at my sister.

"Really?" I asked. I wasn't surprised. Ben was the sweetest guy and seemed to come home with a new friend every time they traveled. "How did you meet him?"

"Oh, we ended up at a fellowship at his house. His name is Jeremy Vuolo." I wonder now if she stared at my face, trying to detect even the slightest reaction or sign of interest. "He's probably twenty-seven or twenty-eight. He's doing pastoral work for a church down in Laredo. And he wears those sweaters you like."

I knew right away what she was talking about. When Jessa still lived with Mom and Dad, she and I loved shopping for the family and picking out clothes for our brothers. I always liked the kind of sweaters with a collar that sort of crisscrosses into a V in the front.

For a split second, I let myself wonder about this mystery guy. I didn't know much about him except that he was in ministry, and he clearly had a sense of style if he liked the same sweaters I like. Jessa obviously thought highly of him. I imagined she thought he'd be a good match for somebody, even if she wasn't necessarily thinking of me. *Maybe?* I thought for a moment longer.

I snapped myself out of it before I let my thoughts wander any further. *Why am I thinking this? I've never even met this guy.* Jeremy Vuolo, whoever he was, wouldn't be interested in me anyway. If he really was twenty-seven or twenty-eight, he'd probably think I was too young. I was only twenty-one, most likely below his radar.

Just as quickly as Jessa had brought him up, she moved on to another topic. *Oh well,* I thought. *I probably won't ever meet him anyway.*

I wasn't in a hurry to get married. I figured I would meet the right person eventually, and I didn't want to rush anything. I hadn't had any relationships with guys so far. No one had seemed like quite the right fit. I didn't only want someone who was tall, dark, and handsome—though those qualities wouldn't hurt. I wanted a man who loved God more than he loved me. A man with spiritual and emotional maturity, who knew how to have a good time but also knew when to be serious. A man who was a leader. I didn't think I was overly picky. But I didn't see these qualities in most of the guys coming around my house.

Because my family was on TV, guys were constantly asking about us girls. Some of them were people we knew from church or the homeschooling community, or they visited our home back in the days when we welcomed fans as visitors. Others were complete strangers who mailed letters and packages to our post office box. I understood it came with the territory when you're a teenage girl on a reality show, but sometimes it was crazy, and a little creepy. At one point, at least twenty-five guys had asked about me or my sisters within a couple of months alone.

I didn't take most of the letters seriously, given that they were from strangers, or sometimes even from men in prison. I'm sure some of them were sweet, well-meaning guys who loved the Lord, but I wasn't going to get in a relationship with someone who didn't know me or anyone in my family. Some didn't take no for an answer. One man drove all the way from Canada to ask my dad if he could marry one of my sisters. Needless to say, he was still single when he drove home. Another guy mailed Jana the strangest packages—a sample-size Yankee candle wrapped in box after box like a Russian doll, for instance. He even invited her on a trip to Disney World, provided she paid her own way.

The guys who knew my family came around our house for church gatherings or events. I liked to sit back and observe, wondering which sister they were here for and what they were really like. I watched how they handled themselves when they lost a volleyball game, how they reacted when somebody disagreed with their opinion, how they discussed their goals and dreams for the future. Most of them grew up in Christian families and shared our beliefs, but when it came down to maturity, they were more like kids than men. Some guys flew off the handle when they lost a game and arrogantly passed off their opinions as facts. Any attraction I might have had immediately disappeared when their immaturity was unmasked. I couldn't get past it.

My parents had decided that if a guy was interested in any of us girls, they had to talk to my dad before they could start getting to know us on a deeper level. Inevitably, after a guy hung around our house, Dad would pop into the girls' room. "Hey, Jinge, so this guy reached out to me," he'd say. "He told me he was interested in you. Are you interested in getting to know him?"

"No," I'd say almost every time. "No, no, no. I don't think so. I'm not interested in him."

I didn't turn down guys left and right for no reason. I genuinely didn't believe there was potential with these guys.

Dad didn't pressure me, and whatever I said was the final word. Not that I never heard other people's opinions. Sometimes he and Mom would say, "Oh, but he's such a nice guy!" Or, "But he comes from such a nice family!" At the end of the day, though, I had to be attracted to the guy and be able to picture myself with him. I didn't feel that way about any of the guys who had asked about me at that point.

I definitely wanted to be married someday. I had always dreamed of serving the Lord with my husband, being a mom, and running my own household. I knew my parents had married young, and I wondered if maybe I would too. At the same time, though, I didn't want to focus on marriage as the end-all, be-all of life. Marriage is beautiful, but I didn't want to look back on my single years and realize I'd wasted those days wishing for what I didn't have.

Once I graduated homeschooling, I threw myself into ministry. I spoke to groups of young girls and took trips down south to visit women at the Florida State Prison. My heart was especially drawn to elderly women. I'd had a passion for serving and honoring widows ever since a woman who we call Nana began visiting our house every single week. She taught all of us kids music lessons and helped our family with the massive task of doing our laundry for fourteen years. I saw the love and care she poured into us and felt something tug at my heart. I thought about how lonely and empty her house must feel, with her husband gone and her kids grown. These women have given so much, but they're forgotten by too many young people. So, I started writing letters, randomly buying them flowers, and bringing them chocolates. It wasn't much, just something to brighten their day and show them the respect they deserve. To this day, I still exchange letters with Nana.

I loved having the time and freedom to reach out when I saw a need. I loved serving alongside my family, and I loved taking trips when TLC decided to send us to London, China, or Jerusalem for filming. Being married and running a house would be nice one day, but for now I was enjoying myself.

And then, it happened. One by one, my siblings started relationships and got married. Each marriage was a blow to me. The girls' room seemed quieter, the dinner table a little emptier. I was used to spending every second with my siblings. Watching them marry off and leave was painful.

But when Jessa left the house, I felt like I was losing a part of myself. I knew it was coming when Ben and the Seewalds showed up at our church and started hanging out at our house afterward. Everybody could see there was something between them, a spark you couldn't help but notice. I saw Jessa blossom from a blunt, no-nonsense girl into a woman in love. I tagged along on more of their dates than I could count, and I knew without a doubt that she and Ben were perfect for each other.

On Jessa's wedding day, I grinned so hard my cheeks hurt as I stood at the altar in my pink bridesmaid dress. I was thrilled for my sister and the love she'd found. I celebrated with everybody else and waved goodbye as they left for their honeymoon in Europe.

It wasn't until I woke up at home the next morning and saw her empty bed next to mine that I felt the full weight of loss. Jessa was my best friend. We'd been inseparable since I was old enough to walk. When she wanted to go on an adventure, I came along. When I needed to get something off my chest, she was the one I talked to. Even a job like cleaning out the family closets seemed like fun as long as we were together.

Our bustling house felt like it now had a gaping hole. *What do I do with myself?* I thought.

At first, I didn't know how often I should call Jessa or drive over to her house just a few miles away. I didn't want to intrude. She was married now, and I knew our relationship would change. No matter how hard we tried, things couldn't stay the same. I kept my distance for a few weeks, not wanting to overstep a line I shouldn't cross. But Jessa was faithful. She and Ben invited us older kids to their house all the time, and they visited Mom and Dad's regularly.

Before I knew it, we'd settled into a new groove. We still texted and talked all the time, and we still went on adventures together. Meanwhile, I'd grown closer than ever to Jana and Joy-Anna, who I'd always loved but hadn't spent time with like I should have. Life was different, but it was good. Still, sometimes I sat on my bunk bed and sighed. Jessa and I had always done everything at the same time, but this time, I was left behind. She got to start an exciting new chapter of life, while I was still doing the same thing I'd always done. I watched Jessa and Ben host Bible studies at their house and focus their energies on serving others. I was encouraged and excited at the thought of doing the same thing myself. *I'm ready to get married now*, I thought. *I'm ready for my next chapter too.*

• • •

The name Jeremy Vuolo came up in conversations a few times after Jessa first mentioned him. I heard Ben talk about the church he helped lead in Laredo, and how he had good theology. Jessa let it slip that he was a nice-looking guy.

Later, Ben said Jeremy planned to meet up with him at a conference. I didn't think it was strange or out of the ordinary. Our family invited friends to conferences, and Ben often ministered to young guys hanging around him. I was excited to meet the guy I'd heard so much about.

The week of the conference came, and my family loaded up our bus for the trip. We'd had our own tour bus for years—it was the only way all of us could travel in one vehicle, and we were used to riding in it across the country. Most of us could even sleep inside it. We parked the bus at the conference campground and climbed out, the stretch of land already crowded with other buses and RVs.

We'd settled in and fired up the grill that evening when I saw a tall guy with dark hair approaching. It was only April, but the Texas heat was already oppressive, and the humidity was so thick I could practically hear my hair frizzing around my face. Everybody tries to look nice and dress up for the week of conference, but within an hour, your clothes are damp from sweat and your hair is limp. I was suddenly very aware that I looked a mess when the guy who said his name was Jeremy introduced himself to me. *So, this is the guy in the sweater*, I thought. *This is the guy Jessa and Ben have been talking about.*

Jessa had said he was nice looking, but that phrase didn't do him justice. I took in his dark brown eyes, his tall stature, his confident attitude. I could tell right away he wasn't like the immature boys who came around our house. Jeremy was a man of wisdom.

I didn't say much to him beyond the usual greeting. It's not that I didn't want to talk to him, but I'm not the kind of person to approach a guy I don't know and strike up a conversation. I hung back with my sisters, grilling burgers and hot dogs and noticing that he jumped right in to play with the younger kids. So many people are awkward when they play with my little siblings, nieces, and nephews, but not Jeremy. He asked them questions and listened to their responses like he was truly interested in what they had to say. He ran around the campground with them, laughing and playing games as if he were one of them. *That's so sweet,* I thought. *This guy is amazing with kids.*

Jeremy hung around Ben and Jessa throughout the week. Every time I saw them, they were either laughing or engaged in a vigorous discussion. I couldn't help but smile as I overheard them hashing out a theological issue. He was a third wheel to a couple of newlyweds, but they were all having such a good time that if they noticed, they certainly didn't care. I didn't join in the conversations, but there was something about him. He loved to laugh and have fun, but he could also be serious at the right moments too.

As the conference went on, I wondered if maybe he was there with his eye on one of us girls. So many guys have come around because of the show over the years, and I figured maybe he was one of them. Ben and Jessa spoke so highly of him that they probably had their eye on him as a potential husband for somebody. I didn't spend much time thinking about it though. After all, I barely knew this guy.

The conference wound to a close, and Jeremy said goodbye to my family before he headed out for San Antonio. It wasn't a memorable moment, certainly not something I wrote about in my journal that night. I figured I might see him again, given that he was such good friends with Ben and Jessa now. Ben is a great friend who keeps up with guys and checks in on them. It was probably only a matter of time before Ben invited Jeremy to Arkansas.

It would be cool to see him again, I thought. He was clearly an awesome guy. He was mature. He was handsome. Maybe he was even interested in one of my sisters. But there was no way he'd ever look at me like that.

Chapter Eight

Strategic Visits

Jeremy

I barely noticed the late hour as I flipped through my Bible. It was long past the time I usually crashed into bed, yet in Ben and Jessa Seewald's living room, I was energized. The three of us, along with another friend they'd invited for the weekend, were engaged in another one of our classic theological debates, and I was all in. I sat in a dining room chair I'd dragged into the living room, leaning over the back as I searched for the right Scripture to clarify my point.

The week at the conference a month earlier had only deepened my friendship with Ben and Jessa. We had enjoyed our time together so much that when they asked me to come visit them in Arkansas, I didn't hesitate. I'd made two great friends, and I was excited to spend even more time with them.

I'd spent my first day in Springdale hanging out at the Big House, which is what they called the house Jessa's parents and family lived in. That night, I headed back to Ben and Jessa's house, looking forward to an evening of lively discussion.

I didn't notice a knock until Jessa jumped up from the couch and opened the front door. Outside, under the dim porch light, I could see Mr. Duggar, his face serious.

"Can I talk to y'all?" he said quietly.

Jessa excused herself and stepped outside. The other friend and I looked at each other silently. Something was obviously wrong. Mr. Duggar could have called if he needed something. Whatever he was saying, this was news he needed to share in person.

Jinger

My hands shook as I pulled clothes off my closet rack and shoved them into a suitcase. I wasn't exactly sure how long I'd be gone or what I'd be doing. All I knew is we were leaving—that night. I felt like an Israelite fleeing Egypt under the cover of darkness.

My brain hadn't quite caught up to the reality of what had happened in a few short hours. Earlier that day, Dad had gathered my siblings and me to tell us that the worst trial in our family history, a trial we had long since dealt with and made our peace with, was now public knowledge. Intimate details about our lives were splashed across a magazine page and all over the Internet for anyone and everyone to read. I felt shell-shocked, as if a bomb had exploded.

I moved in a daze, living in a nightmare that I wished with all my heart wasn't real. One of my siblings had made some sinful choices, but it had all been years ago. It had been awful, but we had dealt with it as a family. We'd sought the Lord, took the necessary steps to move toward healing, and offered up our forgiveness. Now that it was out in public, the old wound was open again, raw, painful.

When the paparazzi camped out up and down the block, we knew it was time to leave. Cameras snapped and bulbs flashed any time one of us dared to open a door. We were trapped in our own house.

Mom and Dad told all of us to pack a few changes of clothes and load up the family bus. We were getting away for a few days until this all died down, they said, to a place with plenty of land to run around outside without anyone seeing us. It would be the perfect place to escape the cameras without being cooped up inside for the foreseeable future.

Dad pulled the bus up, with the door facing the house, so none of the paparazzi could see us loading up. By the time we left, the photographers were asleep, and nobody noticed when the bus pulled out of the driveway and headed down the road in the dark of night.

I leaned my head back into the seat and closed my eyes. The bus engine rumbled and my brothers and sisters chattered noisily, but I barely noticed. My mind raced with questions I couldn't answer. *How do we go forward?* I thought. People outside my close circle now knew details about my life that I had never chosen to share. Details that I had never wanted to share. And there would be fallout. That goes without saying when you lead a public life. I just didn't know how far it would go. What would happen to us? How in the world would we get through this?

Lord, please quiet my mind, I prayed. *I trust you. This feels like a bad dream, and everything is so uncertain, but I know you're good.*

Jeremy

The summer of 2015 came and went. By now, the church in Laredo had asked me not only to oversee the church, but also to step in as its full-time pastor. I moved out of the house I shared in San Antonio and into an apartment close to the church in Laredo. I was relieved to finally be done with splitting my time between two cities and to now share life with the members of my congregation. I was stepping fully into the calling the Lord placed on my life, and it felt good.

I hoped to visit with Ben and Jessa over the summer, but after the bombshell news Jessa learned the night I was there, I soon realized that wasn't possible. The family was caught up in a whirlwind that kept them reeling for months. I tried to encourage Ben as hate continued to pour out over social media, as TLC canceled the family's TV show, and as another shocking crisis hit later that summer involving one of the siblings. Understandably, visiting me was not realistic, especially as Jessa was now pregnant and getting closer to her due date.

Then, I got a text from Ben. They were coming to Houston for an event and wanted to drive an extra five hours to come visit me in Laredo. It would be good to show them around the city, bring them to the church, and host them in my bachelor pad apartment.

The weekend that followed was filled with drives around Laredo and late-night discussions that dissolved into laughter. There was a steady supply of hummus and Triscuit crackers to sustain us as Jessa and I locked horns over a theological topic. I let them sleep in my bedroom while I camped out on an air mattress in my living room, slipping out early each morning for prayer walks and returning with gas station breakfast burritos for all of us.

As I shared my desire for a wife and partner one day, Jessa pulled out her phone. "Oh, don't worry, Jeremy," she said, scrolling through Facebook. "We'll find somebody for you."

I laughed. "Hey, if you know someone you think is good for me, I'm open."

It was a joke, at first. Ben and Jessa giggled as they handed me their phones over and over again throughout the weekend. "What about her?" they asked, seemingly determined to find me a wife.

I drove us to my favorite Mexican restaurant for dinner that night, Taquitos Ravi. Ben was in the front seat next to me, the two of us deep in conversation, when Jessa leaned between the seats and stuck her head in the front. "Jeremy," she said intently, "what about Jinger?"

I leaned back in my seat and thought for a moment. "Huh...Jinger..."

"You guys would be perfect!" she gushed. "First of all, she would be an amazing pastor's wife. She's very caring, very nurturing, the first person to introduce herself to someone new at church. She's always thinking of others and pointing people to Christ. Like, I want to be like her when I grow up."

I nodded, my eyes on the road as I tried to picture Jessa's younger sister. I remembered seeing her in the green dress at the conference, and the way her eyes sparkled when she smiled.

As Jessa told me more about Jinger, I remembered the conversation she and I had the last time I was in Arkansas, when the devastating news about her family broke. While the Duggars hid out for two weeks at a friend's property, Jinger and a few siblings briefly returned for a day to lay flooring at a house the family owned. I was still visiting Ben and Jessa at the time, and when they decided to help with the project, I went along with them. At one point, Jinger and I struck up a conversation about prayer and trusting the Lord in hard times. It wasn't a long or memorable discussion, but what I remembered most was her attitude. Here was a woman in one of the greatest trials of her life, and she wasn't crushed or unraveled. She was sweet, gracious, and hopeful. It was obvious that her confidence was still in Christ.

"Seriously, you guys would be such a good match," Jessa said.

"Yeah, you know, let me pray about it," I said.

The conversation didn't go much further, but I couldn't get the thought out of my head. What about Jinger, indeed? My interest was piqued, especially as Ben and Jessa continued to sprinkle their conversations with nuggets about Jinger's character.

When I had a moment alone, I pulled up YouTube and found a video Jinger had made of her testimony. What I saw captivated me. It wasn't that Jinger was pretty, though she absolutely was. But as she talked about her relationship with the Lord and her journey of faith, it was clear her heart was even more beautiful. I could tell she had a passion to know Christ and make Him known, and that was incredibly attractive.

"OK, I'm interested," I told Ben and Jessa a couple of days later, when they'd already left. "I'll be praying about it. If you could let me know if she's interested too, that'd be great."

"I'll gauge her interest," Jessa said. "There was a guy in Florida who was maybe interested in her, but I don't know if she likes him, so I'll find out and let you know."

Nothing had happened, and yet something was in motion. I didn't know where the Lord would lead, but I could tell He was doing something.

Jinger

I closed the car door behind me as I sat down next to Jessa in her white Grand Caravan minivan. We'd grabbed lattes from Mama Carmen's, our favorite coffee spot in town, before we jumped back in Jessa's car to talk in privacy. The TLC show had been canceled, but we guarded against the possibility of eavesdroppers anyway.

Jessa and I often get coffee together when we're on the go, shopping or running errands. This day in October, however, was something different. Jessa texted asking if I wanted to get coffee to talk. That usually meant she had an agenda in mind. *I wonder what she wants*, I thought as I sipped my pumpkin spice latte, the cup warming my hands on the crisp fall day.

"OK, Jinge." Jessa didn't waste any time getting to the point. "So, what's the deal with this Florida guy?"

I wasn't sure whether to laugh or sigh. I certainly wasn't in a relationship with this guy in Florida, or even talking to him. My family had a connection to his, and while I had been interested in him at one point, the feeling hadn't been mutual. I had gotten over it, but now he was apparently interested after all.

"I don't know," I said simply. "I mean, he's great, but I don't think I'm attracted to him."

"Well, you definitely should be attracted to the person you marry," Jessa said. "You're not just marrying their heart, you're marrying the whole person."

"Yes." I nodded slowly. "I know you're right. But, how do you know he's the right one? How did you know with Ben?"

Jessa's lips curled into a smile. She still couldn't talk about Ben without grinning like a schoolgirl. I listened to the familiar story, a story I was present for as it unfolded. Those two made the sweetest couple, and I truly respected them and the way they handled their relationship.

After a moment, Jessa paused. "You know Ben's friend Jeremy? He's a really great guy."

I laughed. Of course, I knew Ben's friend Jeremy. I remembered him from the conference, and when he stopped by the renovation house a few months later. But I wasn't sure why Jessa was bringing him up now.

"He loves the Lord. He keeps himself accountable to other godly men in his life. He's got great style."

"He seems like an amazing guy," I agreed.

Jessa shifted in her seat and looked at me. "Are you interested in him?"

Her face was half teasing, half serious. I couldn't quite decide if she was kidding. It wasn't that I wouldn't be interested in him. I just hadn't allowed myself to even consider it. He was six years older than me. He was a godly, mature man, with a ministry to run and surely a whole crowd of Christian women lining up for a chance to be with him. There was no chance he would ever look at me that way. I was too young for him. Why should I let my mind and heart wander to a place they shouldn't go? Still, it wouldn't exactly be truthful if I'd said no.

"Well, I don't know," I said finally. "I doubt he'd ever be interested in me."

"You never know," Jessa said. "You're both awesome people. Let's see what God does!"

Jeremy

Less than two weeks later, I boarded a plane from San Antonio to Little Rock, admittedly feeling a bit nervous. Jessa had given me the news that Jinger wasn't already interested in someone else, and since Ben and Jessa were having a big baby shower in a few weeks, they invited me to come. While I was still levelheaded about Jinger, I jumped at the chance. I was single, I could easily get a flight, and I wasn't going to find a wife doing the same thing I'd always done. Why not visit friends and explore a possibility?

So far, I'd met Jinger a few times but hadn't had much of a chance to connect with her yet. This time, my mission was to get to know her better. I wanted to interact with her and talk beyond small talk. I knew she was a godly woman, but now, I needed to know if we had a connection. This was no aimless trip. This was a strategic visit.

Unfortunately, a huge baby shower is not an ideal place to have an in-depth conversation with a girl you're interested in getting to know. I saw her the day before and had a few interactions, and on the day of the baby shower, she was busy taking pictures. I noticed a spunk about her as she smiled and beamed as she took photos. I already knew she was beautiful, but that night, in her long black dress and white headband, she was even more radiant. The string lights illuminating the barn patio cast a warm glow, setting off her eyes that looked blue in some lights and hazel in others. We didn't have a long conversation or anything, but I was hopeful something was there. I was calm. I was collected. But I was hopeful.

"Let's see what God will do," I wrote in my journal that night.

Jinger

I tried not to look at Jeremy too much as I took pictures at Jessa's baby shower. He certainly wasn't the only guy there—Ben had wanted a guy-friendly baby shower, so men and women alike gathered in a barn to celebrate. I laughed along with everybody else as friends and family raced to change diapers on dolls and the guys chugged milk from baby bottles. Every once in a while, though, my eyes drifted to Jeremy.

There was no denying that he was handsome. I was drawn to his personality that I'd observed in group settings, as well as to his maturity and humor. And it was quite the coincidence that he came to visit not two weeks after my conversation with Jessa at Mama Carmen's.

Guys come around all the time, I told myself. *You don't know what he's thinking. You don't know where this is going. Don't get yourself all excited over something that will probably turn out to be nothing.*

Then, I found out Jeremy and I both had flights the day after the baby shower, both early in the morning. I was going back to Florida for another prison ministry opportunity, and Jeremy was heading home. Ben was going to drive Jeremy to the airport, and when he offered to swing by the house and pick me up too, I felt butterflies in my stomach. I wanted to ride with him.

Ben told me to be outside ready to go at four o'clock in the morning. Needless to say, I didn't roll out of bed and jump in his car. Not when I had the chance to talk one-on-one with Jeremy. Normally, I groaned when my alarm went off at 3:30 a.m., but I practically leaped out of bed so I could straighten my hair and put on makeup before I waited outside for Ben.

The ride to the airport was uneventful. Jeremy and Ben did most of the talking, and before I knew it, the twenty-minute drive was over. We said goodbye to Ben and pulled our suitcases into the airport. It was still dark outside, and I hadn't even had coffee yet, but I felt jumpy and excited as Jeremy walked through security with me.

I figured we'd go our separate ways once we made it past TSA, but instead, Jeremy paused.

"What gate are you?" he asked.

Jeremy walked me to my gate and sat down next to me, easing back into the stiff vinyl seat as if he planned to be there a while. My heart beat faster. *He wants to sit with me*, I thought. *He isn't leaving.* I told myself once again not to get excited, but it was getting more difficult.

Somehow, don't ask me how, we landed on the topic of God's goodness and sovereignty, a nice light topic for the early morning hour. I'd gathered from my conversations with Jessa that Jeremy came from a Reformed background. While that wasn't the same background I grew up with, I was excited to hear him talk about the Lord. I listened, interested, as he shared why he believes what he believes. I couldn't help but notice that he quoted the Bible from memory more than once, as if he had a whole filing cabinet of Scripture references he could pull from at a moment's notice.

Something he said reminded me of a verse I'd thought of lately.

"Oh, it's like John 15:16!" I said, going on to quote the verse. "You did not choose me, but I chose you and appointed you that you should go and bear fruit" (ESV).

"Yes, exactly!" Jeremy said. "You know, I actually blogged about this the other day. I have a blog where I write about Scripture and theology. I can put it on your phone if you want."

Before I knew what was happening, Jeremy had my phone in his hands and typed his URL into a web browser.

"Oh, wow, thanks!" I said. Just then, the gate agent announced that my flight was boarding, and we said goodbye. I watched for a moment as Jeremy walked to his gate. Now that he was gone, I could breathe again. This man was incredible. He was beyond anything I'd dreamed of when I thought of my future husband. I was amazed by his love for Christ and his passion for Scripture, by his depth of knowledge and maturity, by his relationship with the Lord that clearly went deeper than words. I couldn't believe we'd spent at least thirty uninterrupted minutes talking, just the two of us, after all those brief meetings before.

I told myself he couldn't be interested, but looking at the blog he'd pulled up on my phone, I realized it might actually be possible. Jeremy Vuolo might like me.

I knew he expected me to read his blog. Anyone else would see it as a chance to learn more about his heart and mind, to find more topics for future conversations. Looking back now, I know I should have read the blog with no hesitation. Yet in my naivete, I thought that simple action would stir up unnecessary desire in my heart. As much as I wanted to, I fought against myself as I stuck my phone back in my purse without reading a word.

Sitting on the plane, I saw Jeremy's face as I closed my eyes. I couldn't deny that I was interested anymore. Maybe it even went further than that.

If it's the Lord's will, I know He'll bring this about in His own providence, I thought.

Jeremy

I floated to my gate on a cloud. I was excited by the conversation I'd had with Jinger. I'd known she was a godly girl, but having a deep, spiritual conversation so early in the morning was great. And she quoted John 15:16 from memory out of nowhere! I was floored. Not only did she know the Bible, but she showed in that moment that she was a woman who wanted to follow God's Word. She was willing to be challenged, and to consider her own beliefs with a healthy skepticism.

Coming to Arkansas, I was determined to find out if Jinger and I connected, if there could be anything between us. Now, I knew beyond a doubt that we did, and that there indeed was something.

"Perhaps you could say, though I am attempting to think only on what is objectively true, that I am a bit smitten by her," I wrote in my journal on the plane. "She is everything I've prayed for. Is this a gift of God to me? If it is, I must believe that, second only to His gift of salvation, this would be the greatest gift He has ever given to me."

I was no longer praying about a general, unnamed wife. Now, more than ever, I was committed to praying about Jinger.

Chapter Nine

On a Mission

Jinger

Nearly two months after our conversation in the airport, I still hadn't seen Jeremy again. Jessa had recently given birth to my sweet nephew, Spurgeon, and she and Ben weren't exactly in the position to host guests as new parents. It wasn't that I was sitting around, waiting for Jeremy to come back. I knew I liked him, but I didn't spend much time thinking about something that might turn out to be nothing. Those two months were a busy time, anyway. Not only did we welcome a new baby into the family, but we also learned that TLC wanted to start a new show with Jill and Jessa, a new show that would eventually be called *Counting On*. And in December, some of my family planned to head south to Central America on a mission trip we took almost every year.

I was visiting with Jessa days before the trip when Jessa casually said, "Oh, did you know Jeremy is going on that trip too?"

My heart pounded. My stomach flip-flopped. In an instant, I realized I really liked this guy. I wasn't only a little interested. He wasn't someone I could put out of my mind. The connection I'd felt in our conversation at the airport was real. Something was between us that I could no longer deny.

I imagined us serving side by side in Honduras, finding moments to talk and get to know each other on the mission field. I couldn't imagine a better way to get to know a guy. Before, this trip felt like just another mission. Now, I was so excited that I surprised myself. I wanted to get there, to be near him, to talk to him.

That thought was followed immediately by another: *I need to repack.*

I'm not usually concerned with making fashion statements on mission trips, but this time, I had packed particularly awful clothes. Even my sisters had commented, "Wow, Jinge, are you really taking that?" as I placed worn-out T-shirts with holes in the sleeves and tops stained with paint in my suitcase.

"Yeah, it doesn't matter," I said at the time. "It's just going to get dirty anyway. I don't care what I look like."

Every hideous shirt that I'd already packed now flashed before my eyes. If Jeremy was coming on this trip, everything had to go. I needed work clothes that were functional but still cute. I had the opportunity to make a good impression and there was no way I was going to waste it.

Over the next few days, as I ran errands and shopped for the family, I stopped by every nearby thrift store and outlet to completely overhaul my suitcase. Finding the right clothes was a challenge, given that it was winter in Arkansas and I needed outfits for ninety-degree weather, but I'm persistent. I even found a nice pair of work boots to replace the sad old pair of Toms I'd packed with a hole in the toe. Carefully, I replaced items in my suitcase throughout the week as I bought new clothes, trying not to draw any attention to what I was doing. I didn't want anybody asking why I was repacking.

I wasn't planning on sharing my feelings for Jeremy with anybody until they tumbled out without warning in my dad's office. We were talking about the trip and I mentioned Jeremy was coming.

"I think I might be interested in Jeremy, but I'm not sure," I said, feeling my cheeks flush as I spoke.

My dad leaned back in his office chair and looked at me thoughtfully. "Oh, really?"

"Yeah, I don't really know," I said. "But he's going to be there."

Dad nodded. "Well, don't get your hopes up or anything," he said. "You never know." It was his classic line. I knew it was his levelheaded way of trying to protect me from hurt feelings.

I didn't let on that I'd repacked my suitcase so I could look nice on the trip, or that my heart raced faster than I knew it could when Jessa had shared that he was coming. I only wanted my family to look at him more carefully during the trip and pay attention to his character. I wanted them to know that he wasn't another guy hanging around. This guy was different. This guy could be the one.

Jeremy

I was filled with anticipation as I boarded a plane headed from Houston to El Salvador. The team would meet up there and then travel to Honduras. This was the week I had prayed about, the week I was looking to find more clarity on a future with Jinger.

After our conversation in the airport a few months earlier, I'd planned to visit Ben and Jessa again in hopes of spending more time with Jinger. But after their son Spurgeon was born, the trip was understandably delayed. Jessa suggested that instead of coming back to the Big House and hanging out like just another guy vying for her sisters' attention, I should join the family on a mission trip to Central America. Jessa thought it would give me more time to spend with the family. I could spend a whole week serving alongside them, getting to know the entire family, and giving them a chance to really get to know me.

It was a risk. The plane ticket alone was $600—not a small amount on a pastor's salary. I also had to miss a week of work and foot the rest of the cost for the trip. And while Jessa told me she thought Jinger was interested, she couldn't give me a definitive answer. It was very possible I could travel all the way to Honduras only to find out she wasn't interested in me.

But I'd seen her character, both in the time I spent with her and in my conversations with Ben and Jessa. I saw who she was, what she was made of. I'd never met a girl of such high character. She was everything I'd prayed for. Someone like this was worth putting myself out there, taking the risk, and trusting that the Lord would direct my path. I'd never know if we had a future if I didn't walk forward. This trip was the culmination of my prayers. By the time I flew home, I'd either have a green light, or I'd close the door forever. I had peace in my soul knowing that no matter how it turned out, I had nothing to lose. Worst case scenario, I'd experience a little awkwardness, but I'd still have the opportunity to do ministry and get to know some good people.

I wonder what this trip will produce, I thought as I gazed at the clouds passing by my window.

Jinger

The trip to El Salvador had never felt so long as it did that December. I knew Jeremy was arriving with an earlier group, and I was dying to get there. I traveled with fifteen other people, including my family members, but I could barely concentrate on their conversations throughout the flight and truck ride from the airport.

Our plane didn't arrive until one o'clock in the morning, and by the time we made it through customs and the bus dropped us off at the host church, it was 2:45 a.m. The gate outside was locked down to keep the fifty-person team safe, and we had to call someone to let us in. I figured everyone inside the church was probably asleep. I most likely wouldn't see Jeremy until morning.

We spoke in whispers and walked on tiptoes as we hauled our suitcases into the multipurpose room, trying not to wake the guys sleeping on thin mattresses laid all over the white tile floor. When I saw one of them pop up and jump to his feet, my heart nearly stopped. It was Jeremy.

"Hi!" he said quietly. He gave me a hug before helping us carry our bags and suitcases full of gifts for the village children.

By the time I settled into the girls' room and lay down on my mattress, my mind was racing. I'm sure I fell asleep at some point, but I don't know how. I couldn't stop thinking about the days that lay ahead. I had no idea why Jeremy had decided to come on this trip, but I was beyond thrilled he was there. *Who knows what will happen?* I thought.

Jeremy

Since our trip was around Christmas, our team planned to bring gifts for all the children in each village we visited. Team members brought giant suitcases filled with toys and school supplies, and our first job was to stuff backpacks with those gifts. The room I slept in my first night in El Salvador was transformed into a bustling assembly line. All hands were on deck as we walked up and down the line of tables carrying backpacks and grabbing pencils, notebooks, and toys for the right age group. Everyone was excited for the week to come and chatted animatedly with one another.

While I didn't go out of my way to find Jinger, we rubbed shoulders multiple times as we crisscrossed the room with backpacks in hand. Once, as we crossed paths, I paused a moment.

"So, hey!" I said. "Did you check out my blog?" I smiled, waiting for her to tell me which post sparked her interest. Instead, she shuffled her feet awkwardly.

"Oh, no," she said. "I didn't get a chance to check that out."

I'm not typically at a loss for words, but for once, I had no idea what to say. Her words were like a punch in the gut. "Oh. Alright." I tried to hide my shock and disappointment as I headed back to the assembly line, backpack in hand.

Game over on day one, I thought. *This girl has zero interest in me. Why am I here?* I had spent thousands of dollars and flown to another country to spend time with this girl, and she couldn't bother to click on the link I gave her? If she was interested in me, she would have at least read the first post that popped up. But to not even click on the link? I had really thought there might be something between us. I couldn't believe I had read the situation so completely, utterly wrong.

I thought of the days ahead and tried to change my focus. I still had a whole week of ministry ahead of me. The trip wasn't a total loss.

Jinger

Everyone was up early the next morning to eat a quick breakfast and load the school bus that took us to our main destination. We had a long drive ahead of us—at least eight hours—to Honduras.

I'd secretly hoped to sit by Jeremy on the bus ride, but I knew it was unlikely. I still didn't know if he was interested in me, and it wasn't in my character to walk up to a guy and sit with him.

I tried not to be disappointed when Jeremy ended up sitting four rows away from me, next to my dad. Most people got up and walked around the bus to stretch their legs throughout the drive, so I got the chance to talk to him once or twice. It was small talk, nothing memorable, but it was something.

Our home base for the week was a church nestled in the valley between Honduran mountain ranges, with thick forests steps away. Roosters woke us each day as they crowed with the early-morning sunrise, the air still cool and brisk. I brushed my teeth outside with a water bottle before heading downstairs. Outside under an awning, ladies from our host church prepared coffee, fried plantains with beans and tortillas, and the freshest papaya, mango, and watermelon I'd ever tasted.

Everybody gathered after breakfast for a time of singing and reading the Word before we were briefed on the day's activities. Then, we all crammed into the little school bus and drove to a village. Since we took this trip almost every year, most of the village children were excited to see us and crowded around as we brought out the backpacks filled with gifts. Someone preached a message, while another group acted out Christ-centered skits to share the gospel. We spent some time talking and eating with the people, and we visited individual houses to take beans, rice, and oil to people in need. Afterward, we moved on to the next village. Serving in a setting like that always draws the team members closer together, and I was glad Jeremy got to experience it.

More than once, they asked Jeremy to preach at the last minute, with the help of a translator. I was amazed that even without any advance preparation, he shared the Word of God in such a clear way that anyone could understand. I loved hearing passion as he spoke. His devotion to the Word of God was obvious, and I could see that he was driven to share it with anyone who listened.

At night, after a meal of fresh tortillas, rice, and beans, team members gathered outside for prayer and discussions. Someone passed a fishbowl around the group and invited anyone who wanted to write down a question anonymously. Someone would then open it up for the team to answer it. The questions were tough, too—some grappled with difficult relationships, others asked what to do about unbelieving family members. Jeremy never jumped in first, as if he had all the answers. He waited until a few people answered and responses had died down before he opened his Bible to the exact passage he had in mind. I was amazed at not only how well he knew his Bible, but also how he could apply it to real-life situations. *This is not something you get just from growing up in a Christian home*, I thought. *He had to apply himself and love the Word of God to study it like that.*

By the end of the week, I was head over heels. I was so amazed at the man he was, his devotion and love for Christ, the depth of his relationship with God. I had never felt such a strong attraction to anyone in all my life. I wanted to be near him. I couldn't help it. It was like a magnetic pull. But I still wasn't sure how he felt about me.

Jeremy

After my initial disappointment, I soon realized I might have a chance with Jinger after all. I'd been around long enough to know when a girl doesn't like me, and I could see she wasn't rejecting me. She didn't shut down any attempt I made at conversation, and she certainly gave me the time of day. A friend of the Duggars named Justin Horseman offered me some encouragement, though he may not have realized it at the time. "I know Jinger, and she's not acting how she normally does with other guys," he told me privately. His words gave me hope. *I think there's something there*, I thought. *I just don't know to what extent.*

Each morning, while everyone was still asleep, I got up early to spend time with the Lord and pray, much of my prayers about Jinger. I found a little gazebo that overlooked the valley and the Honduran mountain ranges, and each day, I brought my Bible and journal to that spot. One morning, I prayed as a double rainbow spread across the sky and clouds in front of me. *Lord, if it is your will, if Jinger is the woman you have for me, please bring us together*, I prayed. *If not, please close the door.*

As the trip went on, the door never closed. In fact, I could see it widening with each day that passed. Spending the week serving alongside Jinger only confirmed everything Ben and Jessa had told me and everything I'd observed in our brief conversations. Jinger never tried to grab the spotlight or be the center of attention. Instead, she went out of her way to look for people in the shadows, the wallflowers, the older women who felt neglected and overlooked in their day-to-day lives. She smiled warmly at them as she sat and engaged them in conversation as if there were nothing else she would rather do. I could see from the light in her eyes and the intensity on her face that this wasn't something she did out of a sense of duty. She truly cared.

As we stopped in villages to deliver gifts and share the gospel, it was clear Jinger was beloved by the people there. She'd visited them many times before, and I could tell from their grins of delight that they looked forward to seeing her. She'd made an impression on the ladies as she invested in them, and they valued her friendship. Every day, I saw more of her sweet disposition and gentle, kind spirit. And every day, my interest grew.

I'd come to Central America wanting to know who Jinger really was. Anyone can put on a nice front and make a good impression in short conversations. There's no hiding your true character when you're roughing it on the mission field. Even on the hottest day, when we were all sweaty and sticky and exhausted, I never heard Jinger complain. There was a joy about her, a humility as she considered others as more important than herself. I could see that she counted it a privilege to serve, even when it was uncomfortable.

But I knew that I couldn't walk up and ask her on a date. I needed to go through her dad. As the trip wound to a close, I knew this was my moment. Before our team drove back to El Salvador, I pulled Mr. Duggar aside.

"Do you have a minute?" I asked him.

He looked at me and nodded, a knowing look crossing his face, as if this wasn't the first time he'd been asked this question. "Sure, Jeremy," he said. "Let's step outside."

I wasn't sure what to expect as we pushed the door open and walked into the heat and humidity of the day.

"Hey, Jinger seems to be an incredible woman," I began. "I would really be interested in getting to know her, but I wanted to ask your thoughts on that."

"Jinger's a great girl," Mr. Duggar agreed. I could see his love for his daughter in his eyes. I waited for him to continue, having no idea what he would say.

"Why don't you and I spend a few weeks getting to know each other first?" he said.

I breathed a sigh of relief. It wasn't a yes, but it wasn't a no either. "Yeah, that sounds great." I didn't know how many times I'd come to look back on the words "a few weeks" and laugh.

Jinger

I felt a sense of dread as we boarded the school bus to head back to El Salvador. I knew that the next morning, Jeremy was flying home, while I would stay for another week. The days ahead without him suddenly seemed flat and colorless.

My spirits lifted when I managed to sit right behind Jeremy for the bus ride. We chatted throughout the drive, and when we made it back to the church in El Salvador, Jeremy invited me and my sister Joy to sit on the back porch and chat with him and a couple other guys. Even though we weren't alone, I felt like there was no one but us two, like we were the only people in the world. We talked and talked about anything and everything as the hours stretched on. I didn't care how late it was, I was happy to be talking to him.

Early the next morning, I woke to the sound of voices outside my window. I listened closely, trying to determine who was talking. My heart leapt when I realized it was Jeremy and my dad. I didn't move or make a sound to give myself away. I could see them seated in rocking chairs outside, both of them engrossed in conversation about Jeremy's beliefs. Seeing them talk like this was surreal. *I wonder if Jeremy talked to my dad about me*, I thought excitedly. *Maybe that's why they're talking about all this.* Their conversation gave me hope that this "maybe" I'd thought of all this time was now a reality. Jeremy was serious about me. I couldn't believe that it was actually happening.

I got to ride to the airport with Jeremy and the rest of the group flying out that day. The ride was less than ideal—we stood in the back of a truck outfitted with bars all around the bed, with a tarp strapped to the outside. We held on to the bars as tightly as we could, practically screaming over the roar of the road, trying to ignore the distinct scent of burning plastic and rotten food smacking us in the face. And yet there was no place I would rather have been. I soaked in those last few minutes together.

Jeremy talking to my dad was a huge step. In my family, you didn't just call or text with a guy when you weren't in a relationship with official approval from my dad. That meant unless Jeremy visited Arkansas, I wouldn't get to talk to him until Dad gave his blessing. But I wasn't discouraged by that, since I was used to that rule. I didn't know when Jeremy and I would see each other again, but I was hopeful.

Chapter Ten

A Love Worth Fighting For

Jeremy

I wasn't sure what to expect when an e-mail from Mr. Duggar showed up in my in-box about a week after my trip to Central America. The e-mail included an attached Word document. I opened it to find fifty pages of questions. Not fifty questions. Fifty pages. My eyes widened as I scrolled through what looked like the longest job application I'd ever filled out. He'd said he wanted to spend some time getting to know me, and this document showed that he wasn't kidding.

The questions weren't surface-level, and some of them were on topics I hadn't yet considered. He asked me everything, from how I became a believer and my position on theological issues, to my opinions on parenting and how I handle finances. They were the kinds of questions that would save married couples a lot of pain and heartache if they asked them before they walked down the aisle.

This wasn't something I could knock out in a few minutes. This was serious, and I approached it that way. If Mr. Duggar wanted to know me, if he wanted me to answer all these questions, I'd do it. A couple weeks later, on my way to visit my parents for Christmas, I answered every single question on my layover from Dallas to Philadelphia. And I doubled that sucker. By the time I sent it back to him three hours after I'd begun, the page count clocked in at 107 pages.

Over the next couple of weeks, Mr. Duggar and I talked a few times, usually on Fridays. At first it was nothing too intense. We mostly discussed some of my answers to the questions he'd sent me. In the Duggars's culture, I had to get Mr. Duggar's approval before Jinger and I could start our relationship. I wasn't too concerned about this—I knew this was how Jinger's family operated, and I accepted that. It was definitely different from how I normally went about asking a girl out. But I saw Jinger's character from afar, and through my conversations with Ben and Jessa, I knew she was worth pursuing. I was hopeful and eager. If Mr. Duggar and I were going to get to know each other for a few weeks, then it couldn't be long before I'd get the go-ahead to start talking to Jinger directly.

When Mr. Duggar asked me to come out to Springdale and visit in mid-January, I boarded a plane and landed in northwest Arkansas, excited to spend a few days at the Duggars's home. Mr. Duggar waved to me from the airport pickup line and helped me place my bag in the trunk.

"Hey, Mr. Duggar, how are you doing?" I asked, shaking his hand.

"Hey, Jeremy, it's good to see you." Mr. Duggar cleared his throat as we pulled away from the sidewalk and drove off from the airport. I knew his house was only about twenty minutes away, and it wouldn't be long before I was with Jinger. It was only eleven o'clock in the morning, and I'd have plenty of time with her before we all attended church together that evening.

Mr. Duggar had a different itinerary. "So, we're going to have lunch with my pastor and talk about your theology," he said, his eyes never moving from the road. "That might be a deal breaker."

I did not see that coming. If anything was a stumbling block, I'd thought it would be my past. I drank and partied in college. I'd been arrested. I could understand parents looking at those issues as red flags. It had never occurred to me that my theology would be the issue. All I could say was, "Oh, alright! Cool!" I wondered what Jinger was doing as we parked in a Cracker Barrel parking lot and headed inside. This day was not turning out the way I thought.

Jinger

I peeked out the girls' room window and sighed. I knew Jeremy's plane was supposed to land at eleven o'clock. Dad should have brought him to the Big House hours ago. *Man*, I thought, looking at the clock on my phone. *Where are they?*

I could barely contain my excitement when Dad told me Jeremy was coming to visit. I knew Jeremy had asked him about me, and that they were talking regularly over the phone. While we couldn't talk or text, I knew I had fallen hard for him.

That January morning, I spent more time than usual in the family closet picking out my nicest top and skirt and fixing my hair in the bathroom mirror. Hours dragged by, as if the clock was actually moving backward. I tried to keep myself busy and not be consumed by what on earth they could possibly be talking about for so long. When they still hadn't arrived by midafternoon, I had to freshen up my wilting hair and touch up my makeup.

I even used the Find My Friends feature on my iPhone to track my dad's location. I located them at Cracker Barrel, and later, when they still didn't come after that, at our pastor's house. *What are they doing?* I thought as I stared out my bedroom window, willing my dad's car to appear in the driveway.

Finally, it was 5:00 p.m., and the winter sky was already getting dark. My heart beat faster when I saw headlights in the distance. *There they are!* It was all I could do not to bound down the stairs and run out to the car to greet them. I didn't want to look overeager, even though the stars in my eyes certainly gave me away. I grinned as I looked out the window, waiting to see this tall, dark, and handsome guy get out of the car.

But no car doors opened. Minutes ticked by as I watched out the window, waiting for them to get out of the car. I felt like an eternity passed and still no one moved. *Come on, come on*, I thought anxiously. *What could possibly be taking so long?*

Jeremy

I unbuckled my seat belt as Mr. Duggar parked in the driveway. It had been a long day and I was exhausted. One minute, I was exiting a plane, excited to spend the day with an amazing girl. The next minute, I was in the middle of long, intense conversations centering on me and my theological position on God's sovereignty in salvation, referred to by some as Reformed theology or the doctrines of grace. While we agreed on the most essential truths about the gospel, that salvation is by grace through faith in Jesus Christ alone, we disagreed on the issue of free will and predestination. The conversations started at brunch with Mr. Duggar's pastor friend, and they continued in his pastor's office, with a few errands run in between.

It didn't take me long to realize I had some theological differences from Mr. Duggar and his church that ran deep. I spent hours laying out my position on theological issues and walking them through passages of the Bible that led me to those positions.

My head was foggy, my mind spent after an entire day of travel and in-depth discussions, but I was glad to finally arrive at the house. Jinger was inside. Jinger, the woman who was the reason for these conversations, the woman who made this entire day worthwhile, was waiting for me. I knew how precious Jinger was to Mr. Duggar. I knew he was being careful in order to protect her. If I wanted any chance at all in pursuing her, I had to lay it all bare before him. Before he could open the car door, I spoke.

"Look, Mr. Duggar," I said, nearly in tears. "I don't deserve your daughter."

Mr. Duggar turned to me, his face serious in the dim light of evening. I could tell he was listening contemplatively.

"I don't," I continued. "She's an incredible woman. She's not gone out and made foolish decisions like I have, while I've wasted years of my life. But I'm a changed man. I'm pursuing Christ."

"I know, Jeremy, I know," Mr. Duggar said.

I could feel my voice about to break as I looked at him. "I don't deserve her, but I'm asking you to give me a chance."

I could only imagine what was going through his head. If I had a daughter, and a guy like me wanted to pursue her, I'd be skeptical too. It wasn't that he was grilling me to be mean. He felt responsible for protecting his daughter, especially since she was on TV and drew interest from a slew of guys who weren't exactly upstanding citizens. I could see he was a kind and gentle man who was honestly wrestling with what was right for Jinger.

"I really appreciate you, Jeremy," he said.

We were out there for at least an hour before Mrs. Duggar knocked on the window. "Are you two planning on coming in? Dinner's ready," she said.

Jinger

The anxiety from the day of waiting melted away as Jeremy walked through the door. Talking to him and being around him felt natural, as if I'd been doing it my whole life. Back in Central America, I'd felt the tension of wanting to be near him but feeling unsure of whether he was interested. Now, that tension was gone. Jeremy wanted to be with me. He'd already spent weeks talking to my dad and flew all the way to Arkansas for me. Any doubt that might have lingered disappeared. I could relax and enjoy our time together.

After he told me about his conversation with the pastor, though, going to church together felt a little strange. I felt awkward as I imagined people staring at us, whispering that he shouldn't be here, that I shouldn't pursue a relationship with him. As excited as I was, it dawned on me that others might not feel the same way about us. If I was uncomfortable, I could only imagine how Jeremy must feel. Part of me wanted to grab him by the shoulders and say, "Please, please don't go anywhere!"

If it's the Lord's will, it will work out, I thought. *God gave me the family I have and put me where I am for a reason. If this is the way we have to enter into a relationship, I know Jeremy will stick it out.*

The rest of our visit was smooth and flew by far too fast. Jeremy was there as the TLC crew filmed us building a tree house in our backyard for the upcoming special featuring Jill and Jessa. Their names were in the title, but I was in the special from the beginning, and the crew visited the Big House regularly. No one told the crew about Jeremy's interest in me, and I laughed to myself as the producer for the shoot asked him to move off camera. *If only they knew!* I thought. *They'd have him front and center if they did!*

Dad seemed to be warming up to him too. On Friday, he even asked Jeremy to lead a Bible study we hosted in our house—on sexual purity, no less. Jeremy told me that afterward, Dad told him it was the best study he'd ever heard on that topic, and that he could see Jeremy had a passion for the Lord.

Jeremy had to fly home Saturday to make it back to Laredo for church on Sunday. We spent his last morning getting coffee at Mama Carmen's with Ben, Jessa, and my mom. We had the best time enjoying good coffee, laughing together, and talking theology—a given if Jeremy and Jessa are together. Mom asked Jeremy such thoughtful questions, and I could tell she really wanted to get to know him.

A few of my brothers and my dad were gathered in the kitchen when we walked through the front door. "So, Jeremy," one of them said, "I have a question for you."

Before I realized what was happening, my brothers peppered Jeremy with question after question about theology. He could barely answer before somebody else jumped in with another question, and then another. I shrank into myself as I stood rooted to the floor, my eyes darting between my brothers and Jeremy. *How will Jeremy react?* I thought. I was nervous. I knew Jeremy's beliefs weren't exactly the same as ours, but Jeremy loved Christ. He served the Lord and dedicated himself to studying the Word and preaching the gospel. That was all I needed to know.

Jeremy handled their questions with grace and humility. He didn't get upset or defensive, and he didn't try to talk over them. He listened, and he answered them calmly and patiently. Watching him remain cool in the hot seat made me fall for him even more.

As much as it hurt to say goodbye, I felt hopeful as I watched my dad's car disappear down the driveway and onto the road. Aside from a few hiccups, the visit had been incredible. My family may have asked him questions, but I could see that they liked Jeremy. I couldn't wait for the day we could start our relationship.

Jeremy

Mr. Duggar pulled into the drop-off lane in front of the airport and grabbed my bag out of the trunk. "You know, Jeremy, you're a great guy," he said, standing on the sidewalk. "But I don't know about this theology."

I managed to keep smiling, even though inside all I could think was,

Really? We'd just had an amazing few days. We had talked at length about every theological issue imaginable, or at least I thought we had. He knew where I stood, and why I believed what I believed. I wasn't going to disavow my convictions for a girl, but I felt I had cleared up a few misconceptions Mr. Duggar had about those convictions. What else was there to say?

If I wanted to be with Jinger, I knew I was going to have to fight for her. But she was worth it. Over the last few days, I'd seen that I had only begun to discover this sweet, spunky woman. When I was with her, I felt a spark and chemistry I'd never felt with anyone else. If this was what it took to win her heart, then I would give it my all.

"We'll talk next week then," I said and shook his hand goodbye.

We talked the following Friday. And the next. And the next. Our conversations stretched on, almost always ending with Mr. Duggar saying, "Let's talk again next week." Mr. Duggar sent me lectures of a teacher he admired, I listened to them, and we discussed them over the phone. Listening to the lectures was incredibly helpful. They introduced me to the framework Jinger was raised in, and that helped me to understand her better. Mr. Duggar never once asked me to adopt the beliefs in those lectures even though he strongly believed them himself, and he was always amicable in our conversations.

Yet months went by and I didn't receive permission to pursue Jinger. We kept up our weekly conversations, and sometimes Mr. Duggar called me with a specific question about my theology. I visited occasionally, which only deepened my feelings for Jinger, but I came home with a heavy heart. Everything I had seen and experienced told me that Jinger was the woman God had for me. And yet, it was out of my hands. I was forced to rely on God with a new desperation. *Lord, I can't control this*, I prayed, pouring my heart out to God. *I give this over to you.*

The godly counsel of wise men in my life kept me grounded, in addition to my conversations with Ben and Jessa. They kept me going when I felt frustrated or when I wanted to give up. I also happened to be preaching a series on the doctrines of grace, the very doctrines Mr. Duggar was concerned about, a providence that kept me fresh and helped me to answer Mr. Duggar's questions with patience and kindness. He and Mrs. Duggar could be my future in-laws, I realized. I wouldn't help my case if I popped off with an arrogant response to their questions. I had to answer in love.

After four and a half months, Mr. Duggar texted me one Saturday morning asking for my dad's phone number. I knew we were getting somewhere. If he wanted to talk to my dad, he had to be close to giving Jinger and me his blessing. Later, he asked for my pastor's phone number, and then my mom's. Dad told me he had a great conversation with Mr. Duggar, and Mom said she and Mrs. Duggar talked for more than three hours. My stomach was in knots as I talked to my parents and waited to find out what in the world was going on.

Finally, my phone rang. I took a deep breath when I saw it was Mr. Duggar. This was it. For better or worse, I would get an answer today.

"Jeremy, I'm so sorry," Mr. Duggar said after an initial greeting. "But I don't think I can let you pursue my daughter. This theology seems to be a deal breaker."

In that moment, I was crushed. Was the entire future I'd hoped for with Jinger slipping away? I'd felt so sure she was going to be my wife. How could it all be taken away just like that? I'd spent over four months talking to Mr. Duggar, explaining my theology and answering questions. I couldn't accept that it was all for nothing. I'd fought all this time for Jinger. I wasn't done fighting. Not now. Not ever.

"Mr. Duggar," I said calmly. "Can we talk about this?"

Over the next hour, we opened the Bible together. We walked through John 6 as I explained that I believed what I believed because the Bible compelled me so. I held back the emotions fighting to come out as I patiently laid out where I stood. Finally, Mr. Duggar said, "OK, Jeremy, let's talk next week."

I hung up the phone, completely wiped. Mr. Duggar had told me no. But then he said to call him next week. What did it mean?

He had said to call him toward the end of the week, so I decided to call him Thursday. Leading up to that day, I fasted, not eating a single thing as I pleaded with the Lord to turn Mr. Duggar's heart.

Thursday came. I was definitely a bit anxious as I punched in his number and listened to the other line ring.

"Hey Jeremy!" Mr. Duggar answered cheerfully. "OK, here's something I wanted to talk about."

My face broke into a grin. We were back on. He had said it was over, but now we were cooking again. I knew we'd reached a huge turning point. *The Lord is so good*, I thought.

Jinger

The months that my dad spent talking to Jeremy didn't seem strange to me. I knew my dad wanted to feel comfortable with the person I married, and I was excited that they had all this time to get to know each other. But when he told Jeremy no, but still Jeremy didn't back down, that made me love him even more. "I don't think this guy's going anywhere," Dad said to me.

The more time that went by, though, the more I realized how many people had very different perspectives on Jeremy than I did. Some friends pulled me aside to share their concerns about the wild life they were convinced Jeremy must have lived as a single man and professional soccer player. The people who talked to me were well-intentioned and only meant to warn me of what they believed were red flags. Still, listening to all these negative comments about Jeremy was emotionally draining. I was crazy about him, and I wanted everybody else to appreciate him too. I wanted people to be as excited as I was. Instead, some were skeptical. *If we get engaged, it could get even worse*, I thought.

"You have to look at the big picture, Jinge," Jessa told me over and over again. She and Ben were my biggest supporters and cheerleaders as my dad continued to talk to Jeremy. When I got overwhelmed, we'd go for walks, get coffee, or drive around town and talk. She knew what it was like to have a relationship scrutinized, and she was there for me.

"You can't expect eighteen siblings to all approve of your guy," she said. "Someone, somewhere, is not going to be happy about it. You already know about his past, and it's not nearly as crazy as it could have been. You don't need to worry about that."

I knew she was right, but I'm a people pleaser by nature, so it was easier said than done. After listening to all the differing opinions, part of me wondered if maybe they were right. What if everyone was telling me the truth and I was making a horrible mistake? What if I entered into a relationship with him only to find out that he wasn't who he said he was? The old fear I'd overcome when I was fourteen crept its way back into my heart. I was scared at the idea of starting a relationship with Jeremy and opening myself up to him, only for everything to fall apart.

Lord, make it clear, I prayed. *Make your will known.*

I told myself not to listen to the negative opinions and other people's assumptions. We weren't in a relationship, but I knew I really loved Jeremy. I wanted to be with him. I couldn't let fear get in the way. In my heart of hearts, I truly was excited, and I couldn't let other people's opinions ruin something beautiful. So, when my dad told me he'd invited Jeremy to join us at a conference, I was excited. This was it. Dad was finally ready for us to start our relationship, I thought. I pushed away the fear lurking in the back of my mind. I could do this. I was ready. At least, I thought I was.

Jeremy

Ben and I were making breakfast in the boys' dorm when Mr. Duggar walked in. I smiled when I saw him. The first few days of the conference couldn't have gone better. I'd spent time with Jinger, and I went out to lunch with her and her parents on what felt like a double date. I came to the campus feeling confident that I would go home with Mr. Duggar's blessing to pursue Jinger. Everything I'd experienced so far confirmed that I was right.

"How's it going, Mr. Duggar?" I asked. He looked like he hadn't slept well. He was still wearing his white undershirt, and his eyes were weary with dark circles. I chalked it up to the early morning hour.

"Jeremy, can I talk to you a minute?" he asked. Something in his tone sent a chill up my spine.

"Yeah, sure," I said. I followed him to an empty room, and he shut the door.

Mr. Duggar turned to me and sighed deeply. "I'm so sorry, Jeremy," he said, his voice thick with emotion. "But Jinger said she's not interested."

For a moment, I felt dizzy. I thought I must have heard him incorrectly. I saw the way Jinger looked at me last night when she told me good night. I knew she loved me. I could feel it. There had to be some mistake.

But when I saw the tears in Mr. Duggar's eyes, I realized he was telling the truth. His words hung in the air like a dark cloud. I felt like I couldn't breathe, as if I had been punched in the gut. All this time, I thought I was trying to win over Mr. Duggar, to convince him that my theology wasn't a problem. I didn't know a much more sinister problem was threatening to tear us apart forever.

Chapter Eleven

Pressed but Not Crushed

Jinger

I was numb as I sat in the empty dorm room. Sitting on the bed, I leaned against the dark wooden headboard and closed my eyes. I wanted to feel something, anything. But I couldn't.

This is crazy! I thought. *What is wrong with me?*

None of this made any sense. I thought back to Sunday night, to the butterflies I'd felt when I saw Jeremy's car pull into the conference campground on the edge of campus. The conversation flowed easily, and I was as drawn to him as ever. We spent most of Monday together, and Mom and Dad even took us out for chicken tacos at a Mexican-Italian fusion restaurant called Stinky Fat Boys. It wasn't a romantic name for a restaurant, but we had the best time. I practically floated to my dorm on a cloud after saying good night to him.

Then, for reasons I couldn't understand, something shifted. As I talked to Mom and Dad that night, I suddenly knew I couldn't do it. I couldn't start a relationship with Jeremy. Something was weighing on me. There were so many conflicting opinions, and I felt like I would divide my family and friends if I moved forward. If I said yes to Jeremy, I would open the floodgates to other people's opinions and criticism. My heart was hardened. It felt like I wasn't myself and something beyond my control was happening.

Now, as I knew Dad was telling Jeremy the bad news, I couldn't even bring myself to feel empathy for him. The room seemed dark, even though it was morning.

Why can't I like him now? I thought. *I've wanted this for so long. All this time, I've looked forward to this moment. Why can't I go through with it?*

"Jinge, what is going on?" Mom and Jessa had asked me. They knew how much I cared for Jeremy, how excited I'd been to see him at the conference. It was no secret in our house that I'd fallen hard for him, and everybody expected us to start our relationship this week. "What is it exactly that's changed?"

All I could do was shake my head. "I don't know," I said with no emotion. "I don't know why. It doesn't make sense. I have no reason for it, I just can't do it."

Jeremy

I practically floored the gas pedal as I drove down the Texas highway. I didn't know where I was going. All I knew was I had to get out of there, away from the dorm room where Mr. Duggar had delivered the crushing news, away from the campus where I thought my relationship with Jinger would begin.

Anger and confusion overwhelmed me. I'd fallen victim to the ultimate bait and switch. If Jinger wasn't interested, the previous five months had all been a wild-goose chase. *Lord, what is going on?* I prayed. *I've wasted half a year of my life! I'm pastoring a church, I'm pursuing Christ, and now I'm getting jerked around. I don't have time for this!* I was ticked.

My thoughts were interrupted by my phone vibrating in my pocket. It was Ben.

"Dude, what is going on?" he asked. "Jinger said no?"

He convinced me to come back to the campus and pick him up. I sat dejected as he climbed in the car.

"Let me talk to her," Jessa said. "There's got to be a way we can fix this."

I shrugged. "Sure. But I've got to get out of here."

Ben and I took off, leaving Jessa to meet with Jinger. We drove for an hour and a half to, of all places, a cemetery. I'd heard that several heroes of the faith were buried at Garden Valley Cemetery, including Keith Green, a Christian musician, and Leonard Ravenhill, an evangelist and author. I had already planned to visit at some point, but it probably wasn't the best spot for someone in the middle of heartbreak. On our way home, we stopped for coffee at a shop ironically called The Journey.

"Ben, take a picture of me sitting outside this coffee spot," I said, "because I've been on a journey."

We returned to find Jessa utterly bewildered.

"I can't figure it out," she said, shaking her head. "She said she's confused, and she doesn't understand why, but she doesn't want to go forward."

I made up my mind right then that I wasn't leaving. If she had said, "He's a jerk and I don't like him," I'd be hurt, but I'd understand. But to hear that she was confused and couldn't do it told me there was hope. If there was some kind of misunderstanding, it was nothing that couldn't be overcome.

My thoughts drifted back to soccer. I'd pursued a professional career nearly all my life until it became clear the Lord was moving in a different direction. In those moments, I'd prayed, *Lord, do I have the faith to stop pursuing this?* At that time, the answer was yes. Now, as I prayed the same prayer about Jinger, I knew I couldn't stop. I didn't have the faith to stop. I didn't know why or how, but I knew I couldn't stop fighting now.

Jinger

I could hear Jeremy in the hall talking to my parents. "Can I talk to her?" I heard him say. I didn't move from the bed, the same place I'd been sitting and thinking for quite some time now.

"Sure," I heard my dad say. "It can't hurt."

Jeremy walked through the door looking somber, as if he'd come from a funeral. I waited as he sat down at the writing desk next to the bed.

"What's going on, Jinger?" His voice was calm but sad.

The wave of emotions that normally would have hit me didn't come. "I don't know," I said flatly. "I just can't do it."

"Can you tell me why?" He looked into my eyes like he was searching for an answer. "We both want this. We've been moving toward this for so long."

"I don't know," I said again. "I'm sorry."

Confusion flashed across his face. I could tell he'd expected some kind of answer that he wasn't getting. "You don't have a reason at all?"

"I feel like our relationship would cause division." I shrugged. "I don't want to do that."

Jeremy looked at me with tears in his eyes, his broken heart written all over his face. "Jinger, I'm willing to fight for you, even if it means fighting against you."

I didn't know what to say. It was the last thing I expected to hear from a guy I'd basically rejected for no reason. "Sometimes I need that," I said.

I watched him walk away and felt angry. Angry with myself for suddenly being unable to like a great guy who I knew was good for me. Angry at my inability to move forward in something I thought I wanted. Angry at my need to make others happy and keep the peace, even at my own expense. My whole life, I'd bent over backward to make other people happy. I was the child who wanted to please Mom and Dad, the sister who went with the flow, the friend who walked on eggshells trying not to hurt or offend. The idea of starting a relationship with someone when I knew that perhaps some in my community wouldn't approve was too much. I knew that, given how I was feeling, there was no way I could move forward with the relationship, and I hated it.

Jeremy

"I have never felt so betrayed in my life," I wrote in my journal early Wednesday morning. I'd barely slept the night before in the dorm room where I was staying. I stuck around, refusing to give up on Jinger even when it looked hopeless to everyone else. Now, in a communal living room, I tried to process my thoughts.

My conversation with Jinger played on repeat in my mind. Calling it a conversation was being generous. I had poured out my heart to her and received nothing in response. It was as if she were made of stone. She didn't act at all like the woman I'd come to know.

Jinger told me herself she was confused. But I wasn't. I saw everything clearly. I knew we would be a good couple. I knew she was good for me, and I was good for her. I knew that whatever she was confused about, whatever she was afraid of, I could help her get through it. I needed her to let me.

"This is heartbreaking for me," I continued writing in my journal. "I seem to have been taken up fifty stories and dropped off the balcony, and by Jinger, the one who was so excited for me to arrive, who gets butterflies when she hears my voice, whose face lights up when I talk to her. Jinger. It's a dagger from..."

"Oh," I heard someone say. I stopped writing and looked up. It was Jinger.

For a moment, I hoped she'd come to talk. Instead, she said, "I need to practice before the conference." She nodded toward the upright piano against the wall. Everything in her tone of voice said, "You're still here?" No apology. No hint of remorse.

"Alright," I said. "I'll move." I picked up my Bible and journal without saying another word and walked to another room. Sitting on a couch next to a window, I could hear Jinger playing hymns lightly and beautifully, as if nothing was wrong. She obviously wasn't bothered by shooting me down and shattering me.

"Coldhearted," I wrote.

Jinger

My sister Jana pulled her car in front of the dorm building and I jumped inside. We'd planned for her to drive me over to the main campus building for the morning session. I was scheduled to play the piano there before thousands of people, but my mind wasn't on songs or the notes. I couldn't shake the image of Jeremy sitting in the living room. Without warning, I burst into tears.

"I can't cry right now!" I sobbed, dabbing my tears with a tissue and looking in the mirror to assess the damage to my mascara.

As we drove, I couldn't help but think how sad Jeremy looked when I walked into the room that morning. And it hit me what I was really losing when I said no to him. It was the first time I'd felt overcome with emotion since I told my parents how I felt. The tears were actually a relief. At least I wasn't numb and cold anymore.

The drive was only a few minutes, barely enough for me to collect myself. *I've got to get it together*, I thought. *I have to play in front of all these people. I can't be falling apart.*

That morning, I didn't notice the packed auditorium as I sat down at the black baby grand piano and moved my hands across the keys. I felt

October 1989, Downingtown High School Track, Downingtown, PA.
As a two-year-old, I loved chasing my dad around the track on his morning jogs. I'd have to wait until I was thirteen before I actually beat him in an annual 5K race on the Fourth of July.

November 1990, Downingtown, PA.
Fishing with my dad. I was three.

Me and my siblings, Valerie and Chuck.

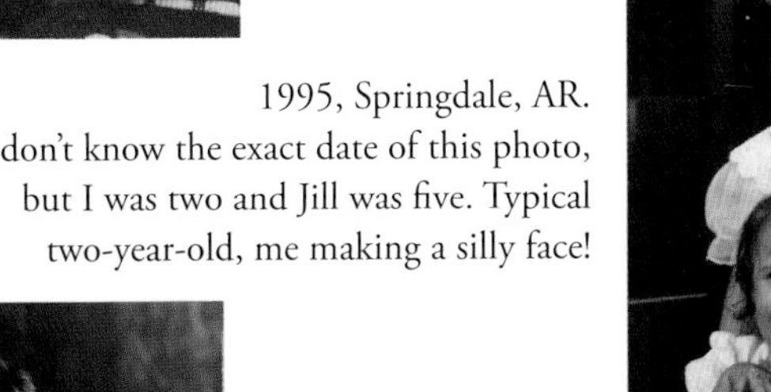

1995, Springdale, AR.
I don't know the exact date of this photo, but I was two and Jill was five. Typical two-year-old, me making a silly face!

September 1998, Downingtown, PA.
Eleven-year-old me on Spirit United Mako Attack, my first "travel" soccer team.

September 24,1998, Sprindale, AR. Here's four-year-old me holding Joy Anna, alongside Jana, Joe, and Josiah.

March 8, 2015, San Antonio, TX. I'd probably met Ben and Jessa ten minutes before this photo was taken. Had no idea this meeting would lead me to meeting my wife!

May 24, 2015, Springdale, AR. Me mid–theological debate with Ben and Jessa, late night in Arkansas. Good times.

May 25, 2015, Bentonville, AR. Getting ice cream with Ben and Jessa on my first trip to visit them in Arkansas.

December 11, 2015, El Salvador.
James was taking photos on the trip taking me to the airport to leave Honduras after a week of ministry. I think he knew what he was doing "capturing the moments" with me and Jinger. Smart kid, or maybe it was just that obvious?

December 11, 2015, El Salvador.
A quick picture before Jeremy jumped on a plane back to the States from Honduras. The next week of the trip wasn't nearly as exciting for me. I missed him!

April 20, 2016, Lindale, TX.
The photo I asked Ben to take the morning Jinger said she wasn't interested in being with me. At this moment, I was perplexed and heartbroken. But I knew I wanted to remember that moment, that feeling. I still had faith that the Lord was doing something, that our story wasn't over.

April 23, 2016, Big Sandy, TX.
Finally together. This was the morning Jeremy was heading back to Laredo from the conference in Big Sandy. I think you can see in my face the peace I felt.

April 23, 2016, Big Sandy, TX.
This was the moment I told her, "I love you." Then we prayed together before I headed back to Laredo.

July 25, 2016, Gramercy Park, NYC.
The moment I asked Jinger to be my wife on the top of a tower with the Empire State Building behind us. As close to magical as it comes!
Photo credit: James Song @jsongphotography

July 26, 2016, Central Park, NYC.
The morning after Jeremy proposed we went to Central Park for an engagement photoshoot he'd planned with James Song.
Photo credit: James Song @jsongphotography

July 26, 2016, Central Park, NYC.
I don't think it had even fully set in that morning: we were getting married!
Photo credit: James Song @jsongphotography

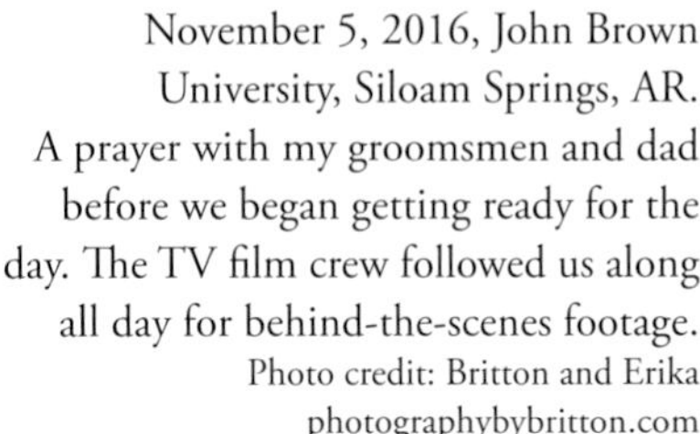

November 5, 2016, John Brown University, Siloam Springs, AR.
A prayer with my groomsmen and dad before we began getting ready for the day. The TV film crew followed us along all day for behind-the-scenes footage.
Photo credit: Britton and Erika
photographybybritton.com

November 5, 2016, John Brown University, Siloam Springs, AR. Jeremy and his groomsmen (from left to right): Joshua Conway, Josue Soto, Luke Booker, Esteban DeLeon, Chuck Vuolo (best man, brother), John Duggar, Dylan Forman, James Song, Ben Seewald, Tim Laughlin.
Photo credit: Britton and Erika photographybybritton.com

November 5, 2016, John Brown University, Siloam Springs, AR.
Jinger's bridesmaids (from left to right): Johannah Duggar, Jennifer Hartono, Jana Duggar, Joy Duggar, Jessa Duggar (matron of honor), Jill Dillard, Josie Duggar (flower girl), Anna Duggar, Kenzie Peters, Valerie Vuolo, Rebekah Kelly.
Photo credit: Britton and Erika photographybybritton.com

November 5, 2016, John Brown University, Siloam Springs, AR.
I remember thinking how handsome Jeremy looked standing on the stage. I couldn't wait to be his wife!
Photo credit: Britton and Erika photographybybritton.com

November 5, 2016, John Brown University, Siloam Springs, AR. The moment we were announced for the first time as Mr. and Mrs. Vuolo.
Photo credit: Britton and Erika photographybybritton.com

November 5, 2016, John Brown University, Siloam Springs, AR. Posing for a quick photo in our getaway car before having to abandon it for the security guard's truck to escape paparazzi.
Photo credit: Britton and Erika photographybybritton.com

November 5, 2016, Siloam Springs, AR. One of our favorite photos from our wedding day. We've printed this out and framed it in our dining room.
Photo credit: Britton and Erika photographybybritton.com

November 5, 2016, Siloam Springs, AR. We found a secluded field to have a photoshoot at golden hour. Our photographers, Britton and Erika, did an incredible job!
Photo credit: Britton and Erika photographybybritton.com

November 15, 2016, Sydney, Australia.
Surrounded by this crazy mob on
our honeymoon!

March 2, 2017, Grace Community Church,
Los Angeles, CA.
This was taken after spending three hours with
Pastor John MacArthur and his wife, Patricia,
during the 2017 Shepherds' Conference.

March 9, 2019, Los Angeles, CA.
Hiking up to the Hollywood sign
in Los Angeles several months
before our move.

June 9, 2019, Laredo, TX.
A bit of early morning sermon review on our last
Sunday in Laredo, Texas, before moving to Los Angeles.
That afternoon, we'd get the tragic and unexpected
news that Grandma Duggar had passed away.

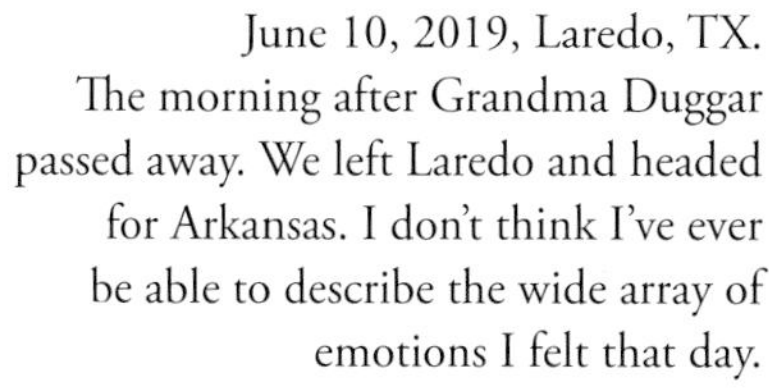

June 10, 2019, Laredo, TX.
The morning after Grandma Duggar
passed away. We left Laredo and headed
for Arkansas. I don't think I've ever
be able to describe the wide array of
emotions I felt that day.

June 12, 2019, Springdale, AR.

June 16, 2019, Springdale, AR.

October 12, 2019, Los Angeles, CA.
Exploring downtown Los Angeles.
Photo credit: Joey Velasquez @_freelifephotography_

November 25, 2019, Los Angeles, CA.
The moment we announced to my family via Zoom that I was expecting our second baby (notice the pregnant Gingerbread cookie). It would be the next morning that I'd learn I had miscarried.

November 28, 2019, Los Angeles, CA.
The days after Jinger's miscarriage were difficult, but there was still joy amid the pain. Here we are on Thanksgiving Day, giving thanks for our beautiful little Felicity.
Photo credit: Madisen Mahoney @madisen.e.photography

as if it were just me and the Lord there, and I played my heart out. Every emotion and feeling I'd bottled up for the past few days came pouring out into my music. By the time I finished, I was drained. *Jeremy is probably on his way home by now*, I thought as I headed back to the dorm.

Jeremy

I'd no sooner sat down at the kitchen table than Ben and Jessa came by to eat breakfast. We were still talking together when I heard footsteps and voices down the hall. It was Mr. and Mrs. Duggar.

"Can we sit down?" Mr. Duggar asked. Their wooden chairs scratched against the white kitchen tile as they pulled them away from the table to sit down.

Mr. Duggar and I looked at each other, our five months of conversations and theological debate hanging heavily over our heads. By now, he could see I wasn't going anywhere. I'd stuck around, even when the situation looked hopeless. And after all those months of talking, Mr. Duggar and I still had a lot to discuss. Neither of us said it, but our faces said, "OK, let's hash all this out."

And we did. We sat down at that table around 8:00 a.m. and didn't move until after three. For hours, we opened our Bibles and combed through Scripture as I answered every question they had about my position on God's sovereignty. We spent probably three hours on one of my favorite passages—2 Corinthians 5.

"The love of Christ constrains us," I began.

"You're always using that word," Mr. Duggar said. "Constrained. Have you noticed that? Where does that come from?"

I was so engrossed in our conversation that I didn't hear footsteps in the hall. "Hey, Jinge!" I heard Mrs. Duggar say. I looked up to find her standing in the doorway, stunning in her long black dress.

"Why don't you sit down and chat with us?" Mrs. Duggar said, pulling out a chair. To my surprise, she sat down.

This was my chance to set her at ease and put her fears to rest. I could explain to them once and for all what I believed, and how it was grounded in Scripture. I didn't want to leave that table until Jinger was confident that we could walk forward together.

Jinger

I could not believe Jeremy hadn't turned around and driven away after I was so cold to him that morning in the living room. Everything in my attitude told him there was no chance I would change my mind. And yet he didn't give up. *Who gets rejected and sticks around?* I thought. *What would I have done if it were me?*

There at that table, I could feel the wall I'd built around my heart coming down. As he talked, a peace slowly washed over me. All the fear, all the oppression I'd felt in my soul began to melt away. I no longer felt the cold contempt that I had felt for him the day before. I wasn't fully myself again, but I wanted to hear what he had to say.

I found myself opening up about my fears, my concerns, and what was holding me back. At this point, what did I have to lose? I told him I was worried that I would divide my community and drive away people I loved by choosing someone from a different theological background. I listened, looking into Jeremy's deep brown eyes as he answered each question honestly.

"Jinger, you can trust me," he said softly. "If I could go back and take away everything I've done that's sinful, I would. But God has used it for my good. I'm a different person now. Ask me anything and I'll tell you the truth."

Other people stopped by to chat throughout the day, but the four of us stayed locked in conversation as if our lives depended on it. Our only interruption was a sweet older man who sat down with us for at least half an hour, making himself at home and showing us pictures of his pool. It was hard not to laugh as he talked, completely oblivious to what was clearly happening among a young man, a young woman, and her parents.

I had been afraid that Jeremy's different theology would push away the people I loved. But I remembered that Jeremy's views were grounded in Scripture. He loved Christ. I didn't need to be frightened of what anyone else thought. Some people I cared about might not approve, but I wouldn't be alone. The Lord had brought us together, and he would see us through. As we talked, I realized that the fears that had gripped me were no different from the fears that used to keep me awake at night as a young girl. The answer now was the same as it had been back then. I had to trust the Lord. I couldn't get lost in the what-ifs that threatened to cripple me. I had to take that first step in faith, knowing I couldn't sink as long as I kept my eyes fixed on Christ.

Jeremy

Jinger didn't tell me she changed her mind that day, but I could see the Lord was working. Her face softened, her posture relaxed, her stone-cold demeanor was gone. She didn't shut me out but engaged in conversation. I had no guarantee that she would decide to pursue a relationship with me, but I had hope.

We agreed to meet back in the kitchen the next afternoon. I wasn't sure what to expect when I arrived. I'd sat next to Mr. Duggar in a session that morning, and when I attended another session with several members of the Duggar family, I noticed Mr. and Mrs. Duggar make a beeline to the back of the room as soon as it ended without so much as a "See you later."

I sat down at the same table where I'd spent hours the day before and wondered what Jinger was thinking. Did she believe everything I said yesterday? Was she still mired in fear? Or was she able to trust me?

When Jinger and her parents walked in, Mrs. Duggar's eyes were puffy, as if she'd been crying.

They took their seats and we picked up our conversation where we left off. We talked for at least two more hours before Mr. Duggar sat back in his chair and sighed, as if he had something to say. "Several things have happened," he said.

Something in his tone of voice told me he was about to say something important. I leaned my elbows onto the table and clenched my hands over my mouth, waiting for him to continue.

"Jeremy, before I met you at the session this morning, I walked behind a young man whistling 'Come Thou Fount' to himself," Mr. Duggar said, looking straight at me. I knew the classic hymn. "The only line he sang were the words, 'Daily I'm constrained to be.' I thought it was interesting that he sang that word after I commented on you saying it all the time."

I kept my eyes locked on Mr. Duggar. I knew he wasn't a mystical guy, and for a situation to strike him as providential, it must have been very significant to him.

"Michelle and I sought counsel with two pastors we trust before we came to this conference," Mr. Duggar continued. "Both of them advised us not to make your doctrine an issue. After a session today, we asked another pastor for his advice."

I realized that must have been why they left the session in such a hurry. I could still picture the speaker, a big, burly man who looked every bit the country preacher he was.

"I told him of our dilemma, and he asked me, 'What does the young man offer a sinner?'" Mr. Duggar's eyes filled with tears as he said, "I told him, 'He offers him Jesus.'"

I stared at Mr. Duggar, in awe of what God had done. I understood that this was his way of giving his blessing. Five months ago, I hadn't believed this moment was possible. There were so many times when it would have been easier to give up, when the mountain ahead of me seemed insurmountable. And yet I knew giving up was not the path the Lord had for me. He never gave me the faith to walk away. He called me instead to persevere. I was seeing firsthand the power of the Lord, the power to change hearts, the power to heal what seems broken beyond repair.

"What do you think, Jinge?" Mr. Duggar said, turning to Jinger. "Is this guy the real deal?"

My heart pounded as I stared at Jinger, waiting for her response. I couldn't even speak as I saw her nod yes.

"Do you want to do this?" Mr. Duggar asked. I was overwhelmed with joy as she nodded yes again. Two days ago, the future I thought I had with Jinger had been ripped away from me. Now, relief flooded my body, releasing the tension I'd carried since the moment Mr. Duggar asked if he could speak with me. I gazed at Jinger with a love I had only prayed for.

Jinger

After two days of intense conversation, we were ready to relax with a good meal. We piled into Mom and Dad's van and went out for a steak dinner at a classic Texas-style steak house, the kind of place with peanuts on the floor and country music in the air.

I was completely at peace sitting next to Jeremy in the cozy restaurant booth. *What in the world was I thinking?* I thought. *This guy is amazing. Why would I say no to this when I want this more than anything?*

As we talked about spending the next day together, a twinge of regret nagged at my brain. I wished we could have skipped the mess of the past few days, that we could have enjoyed the conference together and soaked up as much time as possible. But I knew the Lord uses even our most difficult moments for our good. The last few days were painful, but through them, Jeremy had shown me the true love of Christ. He didn't give up on me even when anyone else in his shoes would have walked away. He was gracious and patient when his character was challenged. I saw the depth of his character and loved him all the more for it.

I was more excited than I'd ever felt in my life for our relationship. This was a true gift of God, and I was ready to walk forward without a shred of doubt in my mind. I knew this was right. This was what the Lord had planned for us. No matter what came our way in the months ahead, I knew we could withstand any test.

Chapter Twelve

Going the Distance

Jeremy

I drove home to Laredo in my rental car completely over the moon. After five months of talking to her dad and a roller coaster weekend, Jinger and I were finally starting our adventure together. It hardly seemed real.

I smiled as I reflected on the last few days of the conference. We had grabbed burgers at Sonic with Ben and Jessa and walked the campus together, talking and making up for lost time. On my last morning in town, Jinger's mom took us out for coffee at Subway, the only place in town open that early.

Before I left, we took a walk down a tree-lined dirt path. It was another hot Texas day, but the shade shielded us from the sun as Jinger and I strolled, just the two of us. I stole glances at her as we talked, taking in the way her long skirt trailed behind her and the way her chestnut hair curled around her face.

"Jinger," I said, "I love you."

Jinger looked surprised. I'd find out later that an early "I love you" wasn't the norm in her family culture. But that was OK. I could see her love for me in her eyes, even if she wasn't ready to say it yet.

We prayed together before I took off. I knew we had to go our separate ways, me to Laredo, Jinger to Arkansas. Our relationship wouldn't develop the way most couples' did. Instead of spending time together in person, I knew we'd have to rely on FaceTime, texts, and weekend visits. It would be a challenge, but like all the challenges we'd encountered so far, I knew the end result would be worth it.

Jinger

Everyone in the house was still asleep when my alarm rang at 5:45 a.m. I sat up and rubbed my eyes. I came from a long line of night owls who loved to stay up late and sleep in. Now, my days began early. Since my house was alive and loud during waking hours, I set up a mattress in the prayer closet. I could get to bed there early enough to wake up at the same time as Jeremy and not disturb anyone in the morning. I'd throw on a cute sweatshirt and pull my hair into a messy bun before my phone rang with a FaceTime call from Jeremy. Each morning, we opened the Bible together, reading a chapter from the Psalms and praying before we went on with our days. Afterward, Jeremy left for his morning prayer walk and sent me videos of what he saw. I loved seeing the mature trees and hearing the birds sing their songs in the background. *I could see myself living there one day*, I thought.

We spent hours listening to the teachings my dad had given to Jeremy back in the days before we started our relationship. We knew we came from different theological backgrounds, and listening to those teachings spurred helpful discussions. Jeremy played the recordings and we listened together through FaceTime, pausing them to evaluate certain points by comparing them to Scripture.

All day long, I texted him pictures and updates of my errands, coffee dates with Jessa, and jobs around the house, while he sent me videos and pictures in between his meetings at church. And we did our best to never miss our evening FaceTime conversations. To the outsider, I may have been annoyingly glued to my phone. But I couldn't help it. I was in love.

I wished he lived close by so that we could spend time together without hopping on a plane. But in some ways, a long-distance relationship was the perfect way to get to know each other. We couldn't hang out with other people or just spend time together. Everything we did involved talking. There was nothing we could do but communicate.

I loved the uninterrupted time with Jeremy on the phone. I loved hearing about his aspirations and goals and listening to his heart. I'd known he had a good sense of humor, but I hadn't realized how much fun he was. He kept me laughing with dry wit.

He encouraged me on hard days, sang me my favorite songs, and mailed me packages filled with the most creative gifts. I'm a hopeless gift-giver, but Jeremy knew exactly what made me smile, whether it was a piece of art made with coffee stains or a necklace with a Starbucks mug on the chain. Sometimes, he sent me letters that were as beautiful and romantic as I could have imagined.

Jeremy visited about every month or so, squeezing in trips between Wednesday night Bible studies and Sunday morning services. During his first visit to Arkansas after my parents gave their approval, our relationship became official—we weren't just getting to know each other, we were boyfriend and girlfriend. As a couple, we decided to follow certain guidelines that were typically part of my culture. That included the rule of not kissing until we were married. As difficult as that sounds, I honestly didn't give it much thought. I knew that's what my family did, so to me, it was normal. Besides, I knew we wouldn't date forever. I wouldn't have to wait too long.

During our visits, we spent our days hanging out with my family, playing Settlers of Catan at Ben and Jessa's, and talking over coffees at

Mama Carmen's—a regular coffee for him, a vanilla latte with almond milk and half the sweetener for me.

Later, I flew with Mom and Dad for my first trip to Laredo. I felt nervous butterflies as our plane landed at the tiny airport. I knew that when Jeremy picked me up, his parents would be with him. From everything I'd heard about them, they seemed like such a classy couple. Their names—Charles and Diana—even *sounded* royal! My family was definitely a little less structured than Jeremy's, to say the least.

I took a deep breath as I saw them standing with Jeremy at the bottom of the airport escalator, smiling and waving at me. *First impressions are everything*, I thought. I was determined that their first impression of me would be a good one.

My nerves quickly melted away as Jeremy's mom wrapped me in a warm hug. "It's so good to finally meet you, Jinger," she said, smiling. "We've prayed for someone like you for Jer, and we're just so excited for you guys."

She and Chuck were so sweet and gracious that I felt immediately at ease. We were still chatting when the airport's automatic doors flew open, the desert heat blasting my face as if I had just opened an oven. *Wow*, I thought. *This will definitely take some getting used to if I live here with Jeremy one day.*

Jeremy's two-bedroom apartment was surprisingly tidy for a bachelor pad. It was pretty sparse, mostly furnished with shelves crammed with books and just one love seat in his living room. But it was homey and clean. I found out later Jeremy's mom arrived shortly before I did to clean his apartment and hang a few framed pictures of us on his otherwise bare walls. I sat on the little love seat as Jeremy played a recording he'd made just for me of him singing what had quickly become our song, "Come Thou Fount."

Jeremy showed me around Laredo, taking me down the tree-lined streets I'd seen in his morning prayer walk videos and the little house where his church met each week. We ate some of the best Mexican food I'd ever had at one of Laredo's many authentic restaurants. As I looked around, I couldn't help but picture myself living there one day, hopefully in the not-so-distant future.

Every time we said goodbye, it got a little harder. The more we got to know each other, the more certain I was that Jeremy was the man for me. He was everything I'd ever hoped for—godly, passionate, funny, handsome—and we clicked without having to try. I didn't want to be Jeremy's girlfriend. I wanted to be his wife.

Jeremy

When Jinger and I started our relationship, I knew that reality TV would be part of it. I'd seen the crews around when I'd visited in the past, but I usually sat to the side if I could help it. But Jinger was under contract and obligated to be on the show. I had to wrestle with the very real question: Am I OK with being filmed?

Mr. Duggar and I went out driving one day to talk it over. He told me about his experience with the cameras, and how a national platform can be positive. This isn't about being famous, he told me. This is an opportunity to share my faith in Christ with the world. While I struggled with the idea at first, I agreed to be part of it. I knew it was something I'd need to navigate wisely, while protecting my ministry in Laredo. As the crew followed me on my visits to Jinger, I got used to the cameras and interviews. They weren't completely foreign anyway, having been a pro athlete.

I already knew Jinger was the kind of woman I wanted to marry when we began our relationship. I was twenty-seven years old, pastoring a church, and at a place in my life where I was ready to be married. The more we talked, the more we connected. We knew we had very similar tastes, but we didn't realize just how much.

We loved to travel. We loved cities. We loved being social. We loved fashion, art, and shopping. We enjoyed classical music and opera. We were true birds of a feather. Her ideal day was mine too. While I knew opposites can survive, and even thrive together, we complemented each other perfectly. Every conversation, every visit, every moment only confirmed the woman I knew her to be, and the couple I hoped we would become.

I was still basking in the glow of love as I flew home after a visit that summer. My flight connected through Chicago, and then I was supposed to fly to Houston before taking a plane to the airport in Laredo. But a gate agent announced that due to inclement weather, my flight was delayed. By the time I landed in Houston at nearly ten o'clock, my flight to Laredo had long since departed. The next flight wasn't until the next day, Sunday, when I was supposed to be preaching. I didn't have anyone lined up to take my place, and it was too late to call someone at quite literally the eleventh hour.

I rushed across the airport to the car rental station and drove away from Hertz in a Nissan Sentra. It was 11:30 p.m., and I had an almost six-hour drive ahead of me. I was already exhausted from the day of travel, but my bed was a long way off. At best, I'd have time to take a short nap before showering and putting on my suit to preach the next morning. I stopped at a gas station to grab a Red Bull and prepared myself to drive through the night.

The road from Houston to Laredo was only two lanes, with a seventy-miles-per-hour speed limit that seemed more like a suggestion to the drivers around me. Semi tractor trailers towered over my little compact car, whizzing by so fast I could feel the car shake. All it would take was one driver to nod off, one truck to nudge over the center line, and I'd be in trouble.

I decided to call Jinger. By now she'd be worried about me, and I knew she'd be awake.

"Isn't that road super dangerous?" she said when I told her where I was.

"Nah, I'll be fine." My eyelids already felt heavy. I took another drink of Red Bull and shook my head rapidly, fixing my eyes on the parade of headlights in front of me.

"Well I don't want you to fall asleep," she said. "Let's talk awhile and I'll help keep you awake."

Hours passed as I crossed mile after mile, each one indistinguishable from the next in the pitch-black night. Yet no matter how late it was, Jinger refused to let me off the phone. She was determined to make sure I was safe, even if she was as tired as I was. I found myself alert and engaged as we talked about our dreams and goals, Jinger's background, and the mundane details of life. A few times, I heard Jinger's voice trail off. She was silent for a moment before gasping, "Are you OK?" I knew she'd fallen asleep and snapped herself awake, just for me.

By the time I rolled into my driveway at 4:45 a.m., I was even more deeply in love with Jinger. That time she spent on the phone with me was another example of her selfless affection. I wouldn't have held it against her if she'd told me good night and gone to bed. Instead, she put my needs before her own, not giving a thought to how tired she was. In the whole weekend together, that was by far the sweetest thing she'd done.

Jinger

After we'd been dating a couple months, it was clear we weren't going to be the kind of couple that waited a year or two before getting married.

We'd already been through a long process before our relationship even began. We knew what we were walking into. We weren't rushing. We knew this was right, and it didn't make sense to us to wait to start our lives together.

We talked to my dad about a time line and, although we didn't settle on a date, it seemed he was OK with us getting married relatively soon. That summer of 2016, I knew an engagement was coming, but not right away. I figured by the end of the summer, maybe in August, Jeremy would ask me to marry him. The thought of wearing his ring, of hearing those words, made me feel excited.

"Oh, let's stop in this ring shop!" Jessa said one afternoon as we shopped together at the mall. *What could it hurt?* I thought.

We'd just walked in the front door when Jessa pulled me to the bridal section. "Oh, wow," she breathed, oohing and aahing over the diamonds that sparkled brilliantly under the lights designed to show them off. Their gold and platinum bands were nestled in white velvet, gleaming invitingly.

"What kind of ring do you want someday?" Jessa asked. "What kind of cut do you like? Do you like white gold or yellow?"

Like most girls, I'd given the topic some thought even before stepping inside this jewelry store. "Princess cut," I said. "I'm pretty traditional. And white gold. Definitely white gold."

A woman wearing a button-up blouse and black skirt approached us behind the counter.

"Are you looking for something in particular?" she asked, smiling.

Jessa got that look in her eyes she always gets when she has an idea. "No, but oh, Jinge! You should totally get sized!"

I looked down at my bare left hand. "I guess that's a good idea," I said. "It's probably good to have that anyway."

I should have guessed the wheels turning behind Jessa's innocent face.

I should have known she was mentally taking note of my ring size and style to deliver to Jeremy later. At the time though, I still thought Jeremy wouldn't buy a ring for a few months.

Jeremy

I had only visited Jinger one week earlier, but I booked another flight to Arkansas. I didn't tell her I was on my way back to see her. I even recorded a video of my prayer walk the day before and sent it to her that morning, before my plane took off, so that she wouldn't suspect.

Jessa was under strict instructions to keep Jinger busy, so they ran errands and drove around town in Jessa's minivan. I didn't want her to realize that I wasn't in my office in Laredo. I really didn't want her to know that I was actually inside White's Jewelry with Ben and Mr. Duggar.

Jinger's family had purchased engagement rings at White's Jewelry for years. It only seemed right that I should get Jinger's ring there too. I felt nervous excitement as I pushed the front door open and heard the bell jingle. The jewelry store felt like an antique shop, with collectibles and memorabilia lining the tall mahogany cabinets. I walked past the coins and old Army uniforms straight to the jewelry counter.

I knew when I laid eyes on the princess cut solitaire that it was meant for Jinger. The man at the counter unlocked the case and handed the shining ring to me. I held the slim band and imagined it on Jinger's finger. I suddenly had an idea. Jinger and I had an east coast trip planned that summer, along with Ben, Jessa, baby Spurgeon, and Mrs. Duggar. Our plan was to fly to Philadelphia to see my parents, stop in New Jersey to see my grandparents, then drive into New York City. While this trip wasn't planned for the purpose of a proposal, I knew now that it was the perfect opportunity.

I pulled Mr. Duggar aside, away from the camera crew that recorded our every move. "Hey, Mr. Duggar, I've got a plan," I said.

Mr. Duggar folded his arms over his blue collared shirt and listened.

"We're going to New York at the end of the month," I said. "What do you think about me proposing to her there? I could do it with the New York City skyline behind us, and she wouldn't see it coming at all. She loves the city. We'll have just visited my grandparents. What do you think?"

Mr. Duggar grinned. "I love that idea."

After ordering the ring, I headed to Tacos 4 Life, where Jessa and Jinger were having lunch. I'd arranged to sneak in the back door to the kitchen and have a tray with Jinger's order waiting for me.

I couldn't keep a straight face as I walked through the dining room to an unsuspecting Jinger. She was so deep in conversation with Jessa that she didn't look up as I approached her table.

"Did you order the tacos?" I asked, placing the plate on her table.

"Yes," she said without even looking up.

When she finally noticed me, she did a double take straight out of a movie. Her jaw dropped in shock as it sank in that I was actually here, not in Laredo like she thought. It was a better reaction than I could have hoped for.

Jinger

I was filled with anticipation as we drove to New Jersey to see Jeremy's grandparents. I couldn't wait to spend time with his extended family and learn more about where Jeremy came from.

Grandma Vuolo was every bit the grandmother I imagined her to be. She taught me how to make her recipe for meatballs as she danced around the kitchen, laughing and making homemade pasta. I adored her right away.

The entire Vuolo family gathered around the huge dining room table for the giant feast we'd prepared. I felt completely welcome as Jeremy's family hugged me and told me how excited they were for me and Jeremy. Aunts, uncles, and cousins told jokes and talked loudly while Grandma Vuolo made sure everybody was stuffed to the brim with spaghetti and meatballs. I was used to loud, given the size of my family, but this was another level. "I hope we're not too crazy for you!" an uncle yelled.

I smiled. "My family's really loud too."

We spent Sunday morning at Jeremy's cousin's church in New Jersey before taking in a Red Bulls game. I loved it, although I didn't understand much about soccer at that point. It was amazing walking into Red Bull Arena and seeing where Jeremy had played. The atmosphere was exhilarating. I was hooked. From there, we were off to New York City. I'd visited the city before, but I was excited to experience it through Jeremy's eyes. He took me down to Alphabet City and his favorite coffee shop, and we visited Times Square and your typical tourist spots, enjoying the city together and relishing each other's presence.

We were eating brunch the next day when Jeremy handed me his phone. "Hey Jinge, look at this." It was a text from his friend, James Song, asking if we'd be up for a rooftop photo shoot during what's known as the "golden hour" during sunset. While we had tons of pictures from our time together, we didn't have any nice photographs where we were dressed up.

"He's a really great photographer," Jeremy said. "Would you want to do that?"

"Oh yeah, that sounds like a good idea," I said.

James gave us an address and told us when to arrive. "Maybe we should go back to our hotel rooms and get ready," Jeremy said. "We could dress up a little for the photos if you want."

"For sure." There was no way I was taking pictures without a shower. We'd spent the day walking miles and miles in the New York City heat and humidity and getting in and out of stuffy cabs. My clothes were sticky with sweat, and I could practically feel my curly hair frizzing like a halo around me.

After freshening up, I met up with Jeremy. *It'll be nice to have some good pictures of the two of us*, I thought.

Jeremy

It was raining when Jinger, James, and I climbed out of the van we took to a fifteen-story building in Midtown. I looked at the clouds nervously. *How long is this downpour going to last?* I wondered.

We dashed inside, trying not to get soaked along the way. "We'll have to wait until the rain stops," I said. "My weather app says it's supposed to let up soon."

Jinger nodded. "If we don't get pictures, it's OK. We can always do it another day."

I kept a straight face as I said, "Yeah, that's true." What Jinger didn't know was on that rooftop, a cellist and violinist were waiting for us. They'd play our song, "Come Thou Fount," as we walked outside as the sun was setting. The ring I'd bought from White's Jewelry weeks before was in my pocket. James would snap pictures and TLC film crew cameras would roll as I dropped to one knee. This was the evening I would ask Jinger to be my wife. That is, if it stopped raining.

I had no backup plan. We couldn't exactly drive to another building with a covered rooftop. And the cellist and violinist couldn't bring their instruments outside if it was raining. Meanwhile, we were running out of daylight.

I tried not to seem too frantic as I looked out the window practically every two seconds. Forty-five minutes passed and the clouds looked every bit as threatening, the rain every bit as heavy. I sighed. *Please, Lord, let this rain stop,* I prayed.

Finally, James glanced out the window and said, "Hey, I think it's stopping."

I didn't miss a beat. "Cool. Let's head up."

We took an elevator to the top floor and stepped through a metal door to the rooftop. Even though I was the person who planned this, the scene before me took my breath away. The rain had cleared, leaving behind a purple sky with a rainbow you could see perfectly from end to end. The skyline of brightly lit high-rises provided exactly the backdrop I'd dreamed it would. Potted trees and plants decorated the rooftop deck, and I could hear the soaring notes of the hymn I knew so well.

We walked together, my arm around her shoulder, her arm around my waist. I looked at Jinger, stunning in her green dress and sweater, certain she must have realized what was happening. But the look on her face told me she thought stringed instruments happened to be playing at the same time as our supposed photo shoot. *Jinger has such an unsuspecting heart*, I thought. It was one of the things I loved about her.

I took a deep breath as we reached the spot I'd chosen. My heart beat faster and faster. This was a milestone moment, a moment I'd imagined since the day Jinger and I started dating. I'd prayed for the Lord to give me a wife who loved Christ, who served God, who put others above herself. I'd prayed for someone who loved children, who followed the Lord's calling wherever it led. Jinger blew all my expectations out of the water. If I'd searched for the rest of my life, I'd never find anyone else who not only exceeded my every desire, but also complemented me in every way. Already I could see she was like a rosebud beginning to bloom, that I'd only begun to discover her personality and humor. I wanted to spend every day of the rest of my life with her.

I had determined I wasn't going to deliver a flowery speech or say anything complicated. I only wanted to say what was in my heart.

I looked in her eyes as I dropped to one knee.

"Jinger Nicole," I said, opening the velvet box holding her ring, "will you marry me?"

Jinger's hands flew to her face. Her eyes widened with a combination of shock and excitement. I could virtually hear my heart pounding in my ears as I waited for her answer. Finally, she whispered, "Yes!"

I slipped the ring on her finger. It fit as if it were made for her. She stared at the ring on her hand for a moment, still in disbelief, still taking in what had happened.

"Are you serious?" she squealed. "Babe!"

I stood and wrapped her in my arms, pulling her into my chest. I didn't want to ever let go. This was the start of our journey together. I knew years lay ahead of us, an untold future filled with joys and sorrows. I didn't know what we would face, but I knew we could get through anything as long as we were together.

"I love you with all my heart," I told her. My fiancée. My future bride. My Jinger.

Chapter Thirteen

"Come Thou Fount"

Jinger

"Alright, everybody open your eyes!"

I stood on a platform encircled by floor-length mirrors. My mom and sisters took their hands off their eyes and gasped.

"Oh, Jinge!" I heard someone cry. "It's perfect!"

"Whoa!" Jessa cried. "This is very you, Jinge."

I stared at my reflection, taking in the dress that hugged my waist and flowed into the most stunning train I'd ever seen. I hadn't imagined a gown this beautiful when I told Renee what I was looking for. Renee, a bridal shop owner from Kentucky, reached out to me shortly after I got engaged, saying she'd be honored to design a dress for me. I looked up her work and was impressed. I liked the idea and figured it was worth a shot.

I didn't give her much to go on, except that I didn't care for satin and I preferred lace. Jeremy told me he didn't have a preference when it came to my dress, but he loved the idea of a long train. It reminded him of the scene painted in Isaiah 6, where the Lord is seated on his throne and the train of his robe fills the temple. Renee told me she'd put together a few dresses for me to choose from, and my mom, my sisters, and I made a trip of it.

The first two dresses were gorgeous, but as soon as I saw myself in dress number three, I knew that was it. The lace bodice and three-quarter-length sleeves fit like a glove, flowing down into a light-as-a-feather skirt that trailed behind in a cathedral-length train. This train made me feel like a queen with its lace edging, and the way it swished gracefully as I walked.

"Jeremy will love this," my sisters gushed. I knew they were right.

• • •

I was never one of those girls who had her whole wedding planned from the time she was twelve. I loved weddings and enjoyed helping my sisters with their big days, but I didn't quite know what I'd want when it was my turn. Since our engagement, my head was spinning with detail after detail. We were on a tight time line too. Neither Jeremy nor I wanted a long engagement, and we loved the idea of a fall wedding. We settled upon November 5, 2016, less than four months after Jeremy's proposal.

For us, that felt like a lifetime, but for people in the wedding business, that was extremely short notice. Not only did we have to find a church that was available, but we also needed a separate space for the reception that wasn't too far away. It also had to be big enough for at least a thousand people, given the guest list we'd already had to trim.

I didn't want just any church. I wanted a church with character, one that hadn't switched over to theater seats and a modern look. The Cathedral of the Ozarks at John Brown University fit the bill perfectly, with its limestone brick steeple, high ceilings with exposed beams, and dark wooden pews that gleam under the light pouring through the stained glass windows.

My mom's friend Cindy took charge as our designer, and I gave her free rein to make our wedding day as beautiful as possible. I wanted her to show off the natural beauty of the sanctuary, using fall colors, flowers, and greenery.

Throughout our four-month engagement, so many family members and friends stepped in to help. Women baked cupcakes and cookies for the reception. People organized transportation to make sure all the wedding guests made it to the reception location. Volunteers spent hours helping Miss Cindy create a backdrop of greenery and flowers for our ceremony. Meanwhile, Jessa helped me overhaul Jeremy's bachelor pad. With her magic touch, his apartment with one little love seat and bare walls except for one Rembrandt painting was transformed into a home that would make Chip and Joanna Gaines proud. I was overwhelmed by the way everyone served us so selflessly.

Jeremy

My alarm woke me early in the morning on November 5. This was a day I'd prayed for, a day that at times I scarcely could believe would come. *I'm getting married today*, I thought. *This is our wedding day.* I didn't feel even a touch of cold feet. I was confident in Jinger. I knew that no matter how she might change over the years, she was a woman committed to submitting herself to the will of God. My nerves were calm. All I felt was excitement.

I'd flown into Arkansas earlier and stayed at a guest house on the Duggars's property, rather than my usual spot at the Seewalds. My parents, brother, and sister stayed with me, and relatives from New Jersey were in town. Having everyone gathered in one place made the weekend feel like a reunion.

I pulled back a curtain, wondering what kind of weather was in store for our day. Outside was like a painting, a pink sky swirled with purple and blue. I zipped on a warm-up jacket and stepped into the crisp morning to head to Jinger's sister Jill's house. It wasn't traditional to see each other before the wedding, but we didn't want to break our habit of morning devotions together.

Jinger greeted me at the door, looking cute in her button-up shirt and skirt. We sat together on the couch and opened our Bibles. The day ahead would be a flurry of chaos and excitement, but in this quiet moment together, we remembered that this day wasn't about us at all. This day was about Christ, and demonstrating the love he has for his bride, the Church. We knew our wedding was being filmed for TLC, and we wanted to use this moment to display true Christian marriage.

After our devotion, I drove back to the guest house for breakfast with my family before it was time to head to the church. Jinger and I were completely in awe as we took in Miss Cindy's transformation of the ceremony space. Greenery covered a wall behind the stage, with white roses and flowers clustered together in the shape of an elegant V. White roses and fall berries adorned the end of each pew, and they matched Jinger's bouquet. It was hard to believe that in a few hours, we'd be standing on that stage, saying our vows.

"I'll see you later," I told Jinger with a grin.

Jinger

The girls' dressing room was a chaotic clutter of hair spray and tangled flat iron cords. Girls camped out in front of any clear space they could find in the floor-to-ceiling mirrors. I sat in a director-style chair as I had my hair and makeup done. I remembered feeling stressed at Jill's and Jessa's weddings, but today, I felt completely calm.

My curls were smoothed and tamed into soft ringlets knotted over my right shoulder, with a delicate crystal headband and a filmy veil tucked into the back. I kept my makeup soft and simple. As I looked in the mirror, I felt like a bride. I'd heard girls say that before but never really knew what it meant. There in the dressing room, taking in my dress and veil, my makeup and hair, I understood.

Before the ceremony, Mom took me to see my dad in a rehearsal room with a piano. He turned as I walked in, looking dapper in his gray suit. He wore a purple shirt to match Mom's sparkling, ankle-length purple dress. "You're so beautiful!" he said, laughing almost so that he could keep from crying.

We hugged and I handed him a handkerchief I'd had made for him. It was printed with a few words to show him how much I love him: "To my dad: You are the first man I ever loved. When you give me away today, know that I will always be your little girl. Your loving daughter, Jinger."

"Jinger, I'm so happy for you," he whispered, tears in his eyes. "This is something we've prayed about for you your whole life. Today God has answered our prayer."

My lip quivered and I felt a sob forming in my throat. I'd always been a daddy's girl. I should have known this was the moment that would bring me to tears. "I can't cry!" I said, dabbing at my eyes with a tissue. "I don't want to ruin my makeup!"

Jeremy

I paced at the back of the church, waiting for the signal that it was time. I still wasn't nervous, but I was anxious for the ceremony to start.

And then, I got my cue. The crescendo of a piano filled the room with music as I walked to the altar with my dad. Suddenly the piano played decisive, commanding chords, and everyone in the sanctuary rose to their feet. This was the moment. I was about to see Jinger in her wedding dress for the first time.

All I could think about were the words James Song had said before the ceremony. "Bro," he said, "don't ugly cry. Cry if you need to. But don't ugly cry."

"Ha! Got it," I replied. In that moment, I didn't think that would be a problem.

But now, as Jinger appeared next to her dad, I knew this was a very real risk. I bit my lip and fought back a fountain of tears as she smiled at me from the back of the chapel. Jinger always looked beautiful, but dressed in white lace, glowing with joy, she was breathtaking. I could hardly believe that she was my bride, that she was the gift God had chosen for me. *Don't ugly cry, don't ugly cry*, I told myself over and over.

Jinger

I felt like I was dreaming as the church doors opened and the music of "Great Is Thy Faithfulness" burst into the hall. A tunnel of people stretched before me, with Jeremy waiting for me at the end. My heart swelled with love as I saw his eyes filling with tears.

I barely noticed the crowd of a thousand people in the pews, or even the decorations I'd admired a few hours earlier. There was nothing else but Jeremy and me. I'm the kind of girl who cries at the drop of a hat, but I was so happy walking down the aisle I grinned until my cheeks hurt.

Jeremy took my arm and led me onto the stage as the congregation sang "How Deep the Father's Love For Us." It felt surreal as we stood before Jeremy's dad, holding hands and smiling at each other. Cameras and giant rigs surrounded us, and my sisters smoothed my train on the stage, but I only looked at Jeremy. He looked so handsome in his navy wool suit.

Jeremy never let go of my hand as his dad told the congregation our love story and encouraged us to love each other even when it is difficult. I loved that his dad was able to marry us. It made our day even more special.

A singer named Latifah Alattas sang our song, "Come Thou Fount," as we lit the unity candle. Jeremy and I had listened to her version of the beloved hymn after we began our relationship. Unbeknownst to us, one of Jeremy's friends reached out to her a few months before our wedding and asked her to sing as a surprise.

We were caught up in the beauty of her singing when we hit a snag. Out of caution, Miss Cindy's husband had wired the unity candles to their holder so the whole stage wouldn't go up in flames. As we grabbed the candles representing our families, we stifled laughs as we realized they were glued to their holders. We nearly panicked, imagining the scene if we accidentally lit the stage on fire. Jeremy tried a candle from another holder without any luck. Just in time, I found a candle lighter someone had left on the stand, and we finally lit the unity candle together.

Jeremy's dad pronounced us husband and wife, and before I knew it, we were married. I felt butterflies as he said, "You may now kiss your bride."

I'd never kissed anyone before that moment. Jeremy and I had talked about it quite a bit leading up to our wedding day. You sort of have to when your first kiss is going to be in front of a thousand people. "Tilt your head to the right," he'd told me. "Just follow my lead."

I should have felt nervous as we leaned into each other, but as our lips met for the first time, any jitters I might have had disappeared. I went for it. Afterward I leaned my forehead into Jeremy's and smiled. Finally. We were married. That first kiss as husband and wife was a relief. The wait was over.

Jeremy

I had to stop myself from running down the aisle with Jinger on my arm. We'd only been married a few short moments but I loved feeling the ring on my left hand, a symbol that I was hers and she was mine. God had joined us together, and nothing could keep us apart now.

Our reception flew by in a whirlwind. Everyone tells you that you barely have time to eat at your own wedding, and that certainly felt true. It seemed we'd barely cut into our naked vanilla cake topped with strawberries when it was time to leave. Jinger and I had opted not to take pictures before the wedding and do a golden hour photo shoot instead that evening.

Leaving the reception hall was tricky. Someone had leaked the date, time, and location of our wedding to the paparazzi, and photographers were camped outside. As soon as we stepped out the door, someone would get a shot of Jinger in her dress and it would be all over the tabloids the next day.

I don't know whose idea it was, but the next thing we knew, all of our wedding guests lined up into two rows flanking the door. They created a human wall for us, shielding us from the cameras. Our guests threw coffee beans at us and shouted goodbye as we ran to the car.

We knew the paparazzi would follow us to the location we'd chosen for wedding pictures, so we needed to throw them off. Our security detail told us to drive around to the back of the reception hall and park it. A pickup truck with a two-row cab was waiting.

"Hop in my truck!" the security guard shouted.

He picked up Jinger and practically threw her in the back of the truck while I helped him shove Jinger's thirteen-foot train into the cab. "Take my jacket!" The security guard took off his sport coat and we draped it over Jinger's dress, trying to cover as much as possible so nothing could be photographed through the windows.

The guard told me to crouch down in the passenger seat. "Hang on tight, here we go!" He slammed on the gas and peeled out of the parking lot like he was a stunt man in a movie chase scene. Jinger and I grabbed onto the seats, gripping them for dear life as we looked at each other and laughed. It was our first adventure as a married couple.

Jinger

Jeremy and I spent a few days in Branson, just the two of us. There was no filming, no cameras, no crew. The best part was we never had to say good night. *I can't believe we're married*, I thought in disbelief. It felt too good to be true.

I was eager to leave for our honeymoon. We'd chosen Australia for our first trip as husband and wife. My family had traveled so much because of the show, so when it came time to choose a destination, we asked the TV crew which continent they hadn't visited yet. "Well, we haven't been to Australia," they told us. Since the only thing we really wanted was a place with a pool where we could relax, that sounded good to us.

Sydney looked absolutely beautiful as we flew into the city. We stayed at a hotel within walking distance of the famous Sydney Opera House, where we saw *Othello* on our first night there.

Throughout the week, we took a boat ride out into the Sydney Harbour, fed a dingo at a zoo, and ate pizza topped with alligator and kangaroo meat. We bought fish at a market and took a cooking lesson from a professional chef. We explored the city and shopped. Even though we were filming parts of the trip for the show, the crew was respectful and kept it to an hour or two a day. Our days felt relaxing, with no place we had to be if we didn't want to go. We could move at a slower pace and enjoy each other.

The plan was to spend a week in Sydney before traveling to Christchurch, New Zealand, and spending a week there. Two days before we were supposed to leave, though, our producer sat us down for a meeting.

"Christchurch got hit with a massive earthquake," he said. "The whole town is reeling from this. There's no way we're going to be able to go there."

I frowned as I thought of all those people hurting, people who lost their loved ones or their homes. The last thing I wanted to do was film a bunch of fun scenes and make light of the tragedy that had taken place.

"So, here's what we can do," our producer said. "We can film a couple more days in Sydney, and you can spend the rest of the week here. Or, after we film a couple days, we can fly to Los Angeles. You can spend two or three days in LA before you fly to Texas." Jeremy and I agreed going to LA was the best option.

My family has made quite a few friends in the Los Angeles area over the years. When we arrived in California, one of the first calls I made was to Ray Comfort, a sweet man who founded a ministry called Living Waters near Huntington Beach. We met up with him and his team our first day in LA. The next day, we went to breakfast with Kirk Cameron and his kids before joining them on a visit to Six Flags Magic Mountain.

We climbed into the rental car, breathless from a fun day of roller coasters, when Jeremy said, "Are there any cool bookstores around?"

Wherever we went throughout our honeymoon, Jeremy made a point to visit any used bookstore he could. We hadn't found anything spectacular so far, but Jeremy was determined to keep looking.

I pulled out my phone and searched for local bookstores. Three options popped up. The first two weren't what we were looking for, but the third option, Grace Books, intrigued us. It was only thirty minutes away from Magic Mountain, close enough for us to make it before they closed at five.

"Let's do it!" Jeremy said.

Jeremy

We were still on our way to the bookstore when it hit me. Some of the Yelp reviews about Grace Books mentioned that it was part of a church called Grace Community Church.

"Wait, Grace Church?" I said to Jinger. "That's John MacArthur's Church!" I grew up hearing about pastor and author John MacArthur, and I'd listened to his sermons over the years. I knew he was a giant of the faith, but I'd completely forgotten his church was in LA. I wondered if maybe we'd get to meet him.

We arrived at the church, which looked like a college campus, with its separate buildings and open-air walkways. A woman working at the bookstore quickly recognized us as we browsed the shelves. "Hey, you're from that TLC show!" she exclaimed. "What are you guys doing here?"

"Well, we'd really like to see John MacArthur," I said casually.

If my request was unusual, it didn't seem to faze the woman in front of me. "You should go ask the office secretary. See if he's here."

It turned out Pastor John wasn't in, but as we spoke with the secretary, Carol, a young man walking by introduced himself and stopped short.

"Hey, aren't you the girl from that show?" he said.

Jinger smiled, looking a little embarrassed. "Yeah, I'm Jinger."

"No way." He shook his head in disbelief. "Let me go tell my dad. He's a pastor here. He'll come show you around."

The pastor did more than show us around. He took us on a tour of the iconic, expansive worship center, with its high beamed ceilings and wooden cross above the stage. It was surreal to stand in the place where John MacArthur had preached for decades. He urged Jinger to play the Steinway grand piano. The notes of "Oh Holy Night" echoed through the sanctuary, and I could see a look of pure pleasure on her face as she pressed the shining keys. He showed us The Master's Seminary and the church's coffee shop, talking to us as we walked and asking us about our church back in Laredo. He ended our tour back at the bookstore, where he wouldn't let me leave without an armful of books he bought for me.

"We really want to serve you guys however we can," he said. I could tell this wasn't a platitude. He really meant what he said. "We have our Shepherds' Conference coming up in March. We'll give you a scholarship. Just come on out. Let us know how we can help you."

By the time Jinger and I sat down to dinner at a nearby Indian restaurant, we were blown away by the experience. It was obvious to us that this church was a gracious ministry that truly wanted to invest in pastors.

"We're definitely coming back," I said. I'd heard about the Shepherds' Conference for pastors, and I was thrilled to have the opportunity to attend.

When it was time to fly to Texas and step back into the real world, I was excited to bring my bride home. I couldn't wait for her to meet everyone at my church and walk alongside me in my ministry.

Chapter Fourteen

The Honeymoon's Over

Jinger

Laredo should have felt like a foreign country to me. It was as close as you could get to one without needing a passport, given that it was a border town where most people spoke Spanish. I'd never lived outside of Arkansas, never moved out of my parents' house, never woken up or gone to sleep without the sound of muffled voices around me.

But Laredo was home because Jeremy was there. No more FaceTime. No more texting. No more wishing he was next to me instead of a whole state away. No more saying goodbye at the end of a visit and counting down the days until the next. We were together, husband and wife. Getting married and moving hundreds of miles away from home was the most drastic change I'd ever experienced. Yet somehow, the change felt smooth. It was different, but in a good way. How could it be bad with Jeremy by my side?

One of the first differences I noticed was the quiet. I'd spent my whole life in a loud and boisterous home. I shared a room with sisters who talked and giggled late into the night. If you wanted to have a serious conversation with no interruptions, your options were Mom and Dad's room, the prayer closet, or someplace outside. Someone was always shouting, practicing the violin or piano, or laughing as they tumbled down the slide in the playroom. Now that it was the two of us in our little apartment, I experienced silence for the first time. *I could get used to this*, I thought.

I'd always looked forward to taking care of my own home, setting it up the way I like it, and cooking meals for my husband and myself. Cooking was a bit of an adjustment, since I'd always cooked giant portions for a family of nineteen people. I was excited to try out new recipes, and Jeremy was even more excited to eat them. He told me he'd only cooked basic meals like pasta with a jar of sauce—that is, when he wasn't eating Chick-fil-A. He would easily eat up to eight meals a week at Chick-fil-A back in his single days.

I could hardly wait for our first Sunday together in Laredo. Jeremy opened the front door of the little stonework building and held it open for me as I stepped across the threshold. I'd seen pictures of the white-walled sanctuary, but being there in person made me even more eager to be there, to partner with Jeremy in his ministry and serve the people of our congregation. Taking on the role of pastor's wife was intimidating, but Jeremy assured me he had no expectations of me. "You don't have to be anything but a godly woman," he told me. "There's no pressure to be anything that you're not."

I'd heard all about the diverse congregation, the people ranging from traditional office workers to border patrol employees. I'd heard about the Hispanic families who'd lived in the border town all their lives. I looked forward to meeting church members, finding my place in the ministry, and welcoming people into our home. I was jittery with nervous energy as I greeted members with a smile, trying to remember everyone's names as they introduced themselves.

My heart swelled until I thought it might burst as Jeremy stood at the pulpit to preach. I'd imagined myself in the front row for so long, sitting under his preaching. Now it was real, and it was even better than the dream. Hearing him preach became one of my favorite parts of the week. I learned something new every single week, and I could hardly keep from smiling as I soaked it all in. Seeing him live out his calling and teaching the Word was incredible. Some weeks, I joined in leading Sunday morning worship, playing my violin as someone else played the piano.

Early in our marriage, we hosted a Friday night prayer meeting in addition to all our other weekly activities. Those meetings were tiny and so special. We spent time praying together before driving to Taquitos Ravi and hanging out for hours, talking and laughing. The food was out of this world, and I developed relationships with a few single girls who became my close friends.

Every Sunday, the church had a potluck after the service, where people could get to know one another better. Each week had a theme, like Italian, Asian, or Thanksgiving, and every family had to choose a dish from a list of possibilities. Usually, I responded to the group message quickly enough to pick a meal I'd at least heard of. If I was late, though, I ended up with a recipe that was common in Laredo but I'd never tried. I felt nervous as I cooked the dish at home, hoping I did it right and having no idea if my results even resembled what the dish was supposed to look or taste like. Even so, it was fun to be part of the group, to try new things, to contribute. I felt loved and accepted, not only by Jeremy, but also by our Laredo church family.

Jeremy

Our congregation was overwhelmingly supportive and welcoming to Jinger. They accepted her right away, and I felt a surge of gratitude as I saw her fit seamlessly into the church as if she'd always been there.

Ministry had felt lonely for so long, but now, I had a partner. I loved seeing her in the congregation as I preached, and when I came home, I could decompress with my best friend instead of collapsing on the couch alone. My days off, which I once dreaded, became my favorite times of the week. We spent Sunday nights relaxing on the couch, binge-watching *The Great British Baking Show* or the all-time greatest movie (at least in my opinion), *Gladiator*. We searched for food trucks and ate full meals for seven dollars total at Taquitos Ravi. We started running together and took up playing tennis.

During the week, Jinger accompanied me to prayer meetings and met with church members. She'd inherited the gift of hospitality from her mom, and she loved gathering people in our house and feeding them, whether it was rigatoni—my favorite pasta—or pancakes and waffles for a Saturday morning youth Bible study. We started a Tuesday night Bible study, and Jinger always made dinner for the whole group.

Meanwhile, our church was growing. Within a year, we'd doubled in size. We had young couples and families with kids, single adults and retirees, most of whom saw the sign outside the church and decided to check it out. The Lord was at work, and it was incredible. We watched as a prominent gang member committed his life to Christ and walked away from his lifestyle, even when it put his life at risk. This man became an outspoken evangelist, witnessing to the men he hired to work for his moving company and leading other gang members to the Lord. Jinger and I watched in awe, completely humbled at how God was using our ministry. Eventually, we had so many people showing up to Sunday morning services that we ran out of space in that little living room. When we needed a new building, the Lord provided us with a church with more than enough space at a fraction of what it should have cost. It was overwhelming and exhilarating all at once.

I'd worried that visitors would flock to the church just to see Jinger, but it turned out that of all the new people who attended, only one family had even heard of *Counting On*. And before long, the father and oldest son in that family came to know the Lord! I certainly wasn't trying to attract fans, but if my wife's fame resulted in genuine conversions and faith in Christ, then that was amazing.

Most people in our church had no idea we were on TV at all, which is how we preferred it. Once, we were at Costco with Jay, an ironworker foreman from our church, to buy groceries and water that we planned to deliver later to a low-income apartment complex. As we pushed our carts loaded to the brim, a woman and her daughter stopped us.

"Hi Jinger!" the woman said. "Uh, could I get a picture with you?"

Jinger smiled gracefully, as she always does. "Oh sure, no problem!"

Jay watched the scene play out and crossed his arms, totally confused. "Why does she want a picture with Jinger?" he asked me.

I laughed. "Let's keep shopping."

Two weeks later, Jay put two and two together. We had a good laugh about it later.

Jinger

On weekdays, I often found myself alone in the apartment as Jeremy visited church members, wrote his sermons, and attended meetings. Instead of flipping on the TV, something compelled me to spend time digging into Scripture. I spent hours with my Bible open on my lap, commentaries spread out on the coffee table, a pen in my hand. Reading the Bible was nothing new for me, but my time in the Word now had a new urgency. Since Jeremy and I had begun studying Scripture together, I had become more aware of the different beliefs and doctrines Christians held. I realized that not everyone interpreted different passages of Scripture the way I always had, and I wanted to find out why. The more we studied, the more curious I became. I wanted to see if the convictions I'd always held were true. I wanted to examine why I believed what I believed, and if those beliefs were supported by Scripture.

In the quiet of the day, I dove into Scripture, poring over passages I'd known for years and seeing them with new eyes. I prayed, asking the Lord to guide me and give me wisdom as I studied. I listened to sermons and read commentaries from Jeremy's office. I dissected the context of verses and strove to understand how the context impacted the overall meaning. When I had a question, I jotted it down to discuss with Jeremy later. "What do you think of this?" I would ask him over dinner or as we relaxed on the couch together. We spent hours dialoguing about what I had learned and discussing Scripture. When it came down to it, I wanted to know what the Bible said. I didn't want to come to a passage with preconceived ideas or try to make the words fit my worldview.

Growing up, I had a set of standards that I took as givens. Now, as I reexamined and compared them to Scripture, my convictions were changing. While some theological convictions wouldn't change, like trusting in Jesus alone for my salvation, I realized I wanted to revisit some secondary issues, like not wearing pants. My mom had always dressed us girls in skirts and dresses, a standard that was taken from Deuteronomy 22:5, which says, "A woman shall not wear a man's garment," (ESV) and I never really questioned it. Modesty was a huge topic in our house, and we believed that wearing skirts instead of pants was a central part of being modest. But I wanted to discover for myself what the Bible had to say.

As I studied, I realized that biblical modesty is deeper and more profound than wearing skirts instead of pants. Modesty isn't only about what you wear. It's about the position of your heart. I wanted to follow what the Bible said, and as I searched the Scriptures for answers, I never found a passage specifically forbidding women from wearing pants.

Once I found certainty from the Bible, my heart was free. I felt no inner conflict as I started wearing pants for the first time. I knew I wasn't disobeying a biblical command. Still, I struggled with believing something that was different from my family. I knew they deeply cared about their convictions, and I didn't want to hurt them now that I didn't share those convictions. I felt emotional as I worried that my parents would think I didn't appreciate how I was raised. I love them, and I didn't want to cause a conflict. In the end, though, I had to walk in truth and follow what I knew the Bible said. We could come to different conclusions about Scripture but still love one another.

My evolving beliefs were challenging and scary all at once, but at the same time, I was excited. I was growing in the Lord and becoming who I was made to be in Christ. I wasn't running from my past convictions, and I certainly hadn't set out to change them. But as I studied the Scriptures, the Lord was leading me through the power of His Word. I saw Scripture differently now. I understood it better than I ever had. The more I learned, the closer I felt to God.

Jeremy

I was caught off guard when Jinger came to me questioning whether she should continue to only wear skirts and dresses. We spent hours talking and poring over Scripture together. My goal wasn't to tell her what to do or make the decision for her, but simply to point her back to Scripture. I saw in her a true desire to understand what the Bible said and do exactly that, just as I had since the day we met.

I understood the journey she was on, a journey to ask questions and make her faith fully her own. I'd done the same thing as a teenager and young adult, when I made the decision to fully devote my life to Christ. Anyone who is serious about the Lord will ask questions eventually, no matter what background they come from. The beautiful thing about Christianity is it can hold up against skepticism. God isn't afraid of questions, and the answers can be found in Scripture, even if they might not be the answers you've always had.

Throughout it all, we drew closer to each other. Everyone had told us that the first year of marriage is tough, full of fighting and arguments as you learn to live as a couple. For us, though, it was the best year of our lives. God knit us together, making us one, forcing us to lean on each other. I couldn't have imagined a better start to our marriage.

Jinger

Jeremy and I were completely committed to the ministry in Laredo. We were energized by the growth and the changing lives we saw all around us. I honestly saw myself staying at the church for years, maybe even until the day Jeremy retired.

Meanwhile, Jeremy hadn't forgotten about Grace Community Church's offer to attend the Shepherds' Conference in Los Angeles. So, in March 2017, he and I returned to Los Angeles, along with Jeremy's parents. Jeremy spent the days absorbed in conference sessions, while a pastor's wife and other ladies from Grace took me around LA to show me the sights.

I was amazed once again by their desire to serve us, people they barely knew who lived in Texas. Everyone we met from the church was on board with the mission of selfless service to the body of Christ. By some people's standards, Grace is considered old-fashioned, with its full orchestra, traditional choir, and grandfatherly men who greet visitors and hand out bulletins. Yet the church practically buzzed with excitement each time we visited, as men, women, and even teenagers waited expectantly for Pastor John MacArthur to open his Bible and carefully explain the Word of God. That kind of passion was extremely attractive.

"Man," Jeremy and I said when we flew home after the Shepherds' Conference. "I wish we could be part of this church!"

"There's no way it will ever happen," Jeremy said. "But it's awesome to visit."

Jeremy

Even as Jinger and I fulfilled our obligation to the TLC show in Laredo, we kept our heads down. I'd gotten used to being on TV, but being on a reality show was still controversial in some of our circles. One pastor even told me not to marry Jinger because she was on TV. Obviously, I didn't listen, but I was still conscious of that tension. Our calling was first and foremost to the church, and I didn't want to do anything to pull me away from that. Jinger and I were terrified of the temptation to pride, that the gleam of the spotlight would pull us away from ministry. We stayed off the Internet and away from social media altogether, even turning down offers for front cover spreads in magazines. Aside from camera crews visiting us every few weeks, we were determined to be a normal couple that just happened to be on TV.

It was, of all things, a financial planning session that changed our minds. Mark MacArthur, a friend from Grace Community Church, worked with us over the phone to help us discern how we could be good stewards of our financial blessings and make wise investments. But Mark didn't just apply the concept of stewardship to our money. He used the term when he discussed our time, our home, and even Jeremy's education.

That's when it hit us. Whether we'd asked for it or not, God placed us in the public eye. He's given us an opportunity to influence people around the world for good and spread a message of hope. We realized then that we had a choice to make. We could be faithful with the platform God had given us, or we could bury it in the sand like the servant in Jesus' parable. I realized we could live public lives and still follow the command of 1 Peter 3:15, to honor Christ the Lord as holy. If people were interested in us, even if Jinger and I still firmly believed we were just ordinary people, we could open the window to our lives and share our hope in Christ with gentleness and respect. So, slowly, without any kind of fanfare, we started social media accounts. We shared about our lives beyond what people saw on the show. As we talked about the future, our conversations now included ways we could use our platform to reach people, like podcasts and books.

Opening that window, of course, made us vulnerable to critics. People on the Internet attacked our motives, accusing us of just wanting to be famous, rich, and popular. But Jinger and I fully recognized that faithful stewardship is not always the easiest way. It's easy to be a recluse. The question we were asking wasn't which path was easier, but which path was more faithful. How would we be able to impact the most people the most powerfully?

Meanwhile, our connection to Grace Church continued to grow. The first time anyone mentioned seminary to me, I was giving my testimony at a Grace Church staff chapel. The church had invited us down in August 2017, and Jinger and I were only too happy to have another excuse to visit.

I was sitting on the stage when someone asked, "So, you're coming to seminary, right?"

"Oh, yeah, thank you so much for that full-ride scholarship," I deadpanned. I got a good laugh from the crowd, but afterward, a Master's Seminary administrator asked me to have coffee with him.

"Have you ever considered seminary?" he asked me after we'd ordered.

Of course, I'd thought about it. I wanted to deepen my understanding of the Word and become a better pastor, but I was already leading the church in Laredo. As many wonderful things as I'd heard about The Master's Seminary, I couldn't leave my church. I shook the administrator's hand afterward and figured that was that.

Jinger and I felt more connected to Grace each time we visited. I was amazed by the humility and servant's heart of Pastor John, who at nearly eighty years old still preached almost every Sunday. Millions of people all over the world listen to this man's sermons, yet when I was first introduced to him as a pastor, he gave me a thumbs-up and said, "We're partners."

Pastor John invited Jinger and me to have lunch with him and his wife, Patricia, during the Shepherds' Conference. That week is easily his busiest week of the year, but as we sat in his office eating food he'd had delivered, he didn't even glance at a clock. He spent three hours with us, encouraging us and discussing how to walk with conviction. We talked theology, we talked about our journeys, our lives, our faith. I thought I would be intimidated talking to him—someone I've always considered a hero of the faith—but he was nothing but congenial and warm.

When he finally excused himself and returned to the conference, one of the pastors looked at us in shock. "What just happened?" he said. "I've never seen him spend three hours with anybody, let alone during Shepherds' Conference."

I realized what a beautiful privilege we'd experienced. We felt completely welcomed and loved by the church, as if we were at home. This church didn't need us at all, but the people there were interested in us anyway. The more I felt our connection growing, the more I wished we could be part of this world.

But a cross-country move wasn't something we saw in our future. Not yet, anyway. Not when we had just learned that soon it wouldn't be just the two of us anymore.

Chapter Fifteen

Of Colic and Midnight Feedings

Jeremy

I'd always known I wanted to be a dad. Kids somehow seem to know that despite my stature and facial hair, I'm on their level. By the time Jinger and I got married, I was at an age where I was ready for a baby, and we knew we wanted to have a few kids one day.

But I also knew that we needed to wait. Our whole relationship had been fast-paced, and Jinger had only recently experienced the most drastic changes of her life. We needed to slow down and take a year to get to know each other as husband and wife before we had kids.

In the meantime, we decided it was time for a house. I took Jinger house hunting on a whim one Sunday after finding a place online that looked promising. As we navigated the neighborhood streets, searching for the house number from the listing, we noticed another house with a "For Sale By Owner" sign in front of it. The tan brick ranch house had big windows overlooking the lush front yard, with a stately mature tree providing much-needed shade from the Texas heat.

We looked at several other houses, but in the end, nothing compared to that house we'd noticed from the street. The four-bedroom, two-bath house needed a little paint, but its high ceilings and spacious rooms with white-tiled floors were perfect for us. Within a couple months, we moved out of our apartment and settled into our first house.

It was only a couple months later that Jinger touched my arm, a tender look on her face. "Jer, I think I'm ready," she said. "Let's have a baby."

Jinger

I was never the kind of girl who was always offering to babysit or asking to hold babies. I was happy to comb my little sisters' hair or help my younger siblings with their music lessons. I liked kids, but the thought of having a child of my own made me nervous. How in the world would I take care of a kid twenty-four hours a day, seven days a week?

Then, as months passed, something changed. I could feel it when I watched Jeremy wrestling and playing with my nephew, Spurgeon. I couldn't wait to see him hold our own baby one day and watch him loving on our child.

As I held a friend's newborn one day, I knew I was ready. I nuzzled the little one's downy head to my cheek and felt her tiny fingers close around mine. *Maybe this isn't so scary*, I thought. *I can do this. I know I can.*

We were celebrating our first anniversary in San Antonio when I took a pregnancy test in our River Walk hotel room. Jeremy was on the phone in the next room as I watched two pink lines slowly appear on the stick in my hand. Two pink lines that would change our lives forever. It felt like I was dreaming. I grinned as I stared at the stick, trying to assure myself that the lines were really there.

I waited in the bathroom, impatient for Jeremy to get off the phone so I could tell him the good news. *Oh, my goodness, when is this conversation going to end?* I thought.

When I heard him finally say goodbye, I opened the door. "Hey, I have another gift for you!"

He looked up from his phone, confused. We'd already exchanged gifts the day before. "What is it?"

I didn't say a word as I handed him the test.

We celebrated the news with a fancy dinner at the Tower of the Americas restaurant, with stunning views of the glittering city on that beautiful fall evening. It didn't feel real that life was growing inside me right at that moment.

Jeremy

As excited as I was about the baby, the reality of it didn't set in at first. While Jinger was experiencing morning sickness and fatigue, nothing had changed for me. I tried to help by running out to get Jinger any food that sounded remotely palatable or buying her every variety of sparkling water known to man when regular water made her nauseated. I spent a lot of time in prayer for our baby and asking that he or she would look and act like Jinger. Seriously.

But when we had our first ultrasound halfway through the pregnancy, it finally sank in. We'd decided to have the baby in San Antonio and had to drive two and a half hours for every doctor's visit. The film crew was there as the ultrasound technician squirted a cold clear jelly on Jinger's belly and moved a probe around her abdomen. I was breathless as I watched the screen and the technician pointed out our little one's head, hands, and feet. *Wow*, I thought, marveling at the little gray blob squirming around. *That's my baby.*

Once the technician assured us that Baby Vuolo was healthy, there was still one very important piece of information left. We waited anxiously as the technician studied the screen, then smiled. "It's a girl!"

I was completely overjoyed that a little princess was on her way. I imagined us playing soccer in the backyard, reading her my favorite Bible stories, taking her on daddy-daughter dates. I couldn't wait.

We kept the baby's gender a secret for a few weeks until our families flew out to Laredo for a reveal party. Our baby was the twelfth grandchild on Jinger's side, and her brothers and sisters had used every traditional gender reveal method. So, we got creative. We set up an elaborate obstacle course in our backyard that ended with a neon sign that said "Baby." We divided our families into two teams—Team Girl and Team Boy—and the winning team would get to pull a string lighting up the sign, revealing the gender.

Everyone had to eat a cup of ice cream before placing their heads on a plastic bat and spinning ten times. Then, they had to hop on a bouncy ball, crawl through a tunnel, use a Hula-Hoop, and on and on. We were not messing around with that obstacle course. In retrospect, forcing everyone to eat ice cream before spinning on a bat was a bad plan. Jinger had warned me that her family gets motion sickness, and I learned that day that she definitely wasn't kidding. But everyone shouted with excitement when the sign lit up bright pink and Jinger and I sprayed our family with pink Silly String.

Jinger

By July, with our July 20 due date rapidly approaching, I could hardly wait for the baby to arrive. My sisters visited and helped me decorate the baby's room in a southwestern theme, with a white-and-natural wood crib, gray walls, and a cute cactus painting. I was a little nervous about the birth, given the complications some of my sisters had experienced with their nine- and ten-pound babies. I started taking natural herbs under the supervision of my midwife, took long walks, and ate spicy foods, all in hopes that I could get labor going a little early and better my chances of a smooth birth. We also stayed at a San Antonio hotel a few days before my due date so that we could avoid making the two-and-a-half-hour drive from Laredo while I was in labor.

When my midwife checked me and saw that my body was showing early signs of labor, she recommended that I head to the hospital to induce labor. My heart pounded as we climbed into the car. I'd imagined the day I went into labor, but now that it was here, it felt surreal. My sisters' stories of pain and complications flashed through my head. *Oh my*, I thought. *How is this going to go?* We settled into our spacious labor suite and I put on the blue polka-dot laboring gown I'd bought. The doctors started me on some gentle induction methods to slowly ease my body into labor.

After having regular contractions through the night, the doctor started me on a Pitocin drip. My mom and Jana, whom I'd asked to be at the hospital, did jigsaw puzzles and talked with me to pass the time. As hours crept by and my body wasn't progressing, I felt even more nervous. I knew that a healthy baby was all that mattered, but I really wanted to avoid a C-section. My midwife helped me get into positions that eased the pressure on my lower back. When my doctor increased the Pitocin, the contractions intensified, squeezing my belly in an iron grip that had me doubled over in pain. The mood in my delivery room intensified. For seven hours, the contractions came like clockwork, waking me whenever I managed to fall asleep. Tears of pain and frustration rolled down my cheeks. I was sweaty, exhausted, and completely spent. *I can't do this. I'm so tired. I have to sleep!* Jeremy rubbed my back and prayed with me.

I decided to get an epidural. The anesthesiologist had barely left the room when all the pain disappeared. "Why didn't I do this earlier?" I said. "I feel great!"

With my body finally relaxed, I collapsed into sleep. Nurses checked on me every thirty minutes, rolling me from one side to the other, but I was so conked out I didn't even notice. When I awoke at 3:00 a.m., I felt rested and ready for what lay ahead.

"Let's see if you've made any progress," a nurse said when she saw I was awake. I watched her face change in surprise. "Oh wow! How are you feeling?"

I shrugged. "I don't feel any different."

The nurse took off her gloves in a hurry. "If you feel any pressure, do NOT push." She ran out of the room before I could ask what she was talking about.

My mom, who slept on the couch next to me the whole time, sat up and smiled sweetly.

"Hey, Jinge," she said in her calm, soothing voice. "You're doing great. The baby's going to be here real soon."

The next few minutes were like a whirlwind. The quiet delivery room sprang to life as it filled with my sisters, my friend Laura, Jeremy's mom, and the nurses. My midwife prepped me for what was about to happen before the doctor breezed in.

I held Jeremy's hand and pushed. Everything was a blur as I focused on this last hurdle that stood between me and my baby. A few more pushes and my life would change forever. A few more pushes and my baby would be in my arms. Time moved in slow motion. Instincts I didn't know I had took over. I forgot about everybody else in the room as I focused all I had left on bringing this baby into the world. The words of encouragement, the doctor's instructions, everything melted into the background. There was nothing but me and the task still before me, the job that no one but me could accomplish right now. Almost there. Almost there.

And then, she was here. I fell back onto the pillow, indescribable joy and relief washing over me as I heard Felicity Nicole cry out at 4:37 a.m.

"You did it, Jinge!"

"A baby girl!"

"Oh, my goodness!"

Felicity was puffy and covered in goo when the doctor laid her on my chest, and I thought she was the sweetest thing I'd ever seen. Jeremy knelt down to kiss me before he stroked our new daughter's head. My eyes filled with tears at the sight of him overcome with love for our baby.

"We love you," I whispered to Felicity. "We've been praying for you." It was the most precious moment of my life.

Jeremy

A buddy of mine had sarcastically warned me that watching your baby being born is like watching an alien dying. I was prepared for the scariest moment of my life. Instead, I felt helpless in the delivery room as I watched Jinger writhe in pain, powerless to do anything but pray for her and comfort her. When she laid her head on my chest in tears, I cried with her.

But when I held my daughter in my arms, she didn't look anything like an alien to me. She was absolutely beautiful, even though Jana had the nerve to tell me our daughter looked like me after I prayed for her to look like Jinger. "How dare you!" I said jokingly.

I was in awe of my wife. I had always appreciated her, but after watching the body-and-soul effort she put into bringing our baby into the world, my appreciation for her, as well as for my mom, went through the roof.

We kept Felicity's name a surprise until she was born. We chose the name in honor of Felicitas, a Christian martyr who was pregnant at the time she was sentenced to death. Her story is gripping and powerful, a story of courage and enduring faith. When we learned the name Felicity means "happiness," that sealed the deal. Looking at our little eight-pound angel now, her name certainly fit. We never considered naming her with a *J* name, especially since all the good names were taken by Jinger's family. If we were going to do biblical names that started with a *J*, basically the only names left were Jezebel and Judas. And yes, that is a terrible dad joke.

After Felicity's birth, our mother-baby suite was filled with family members, gushing and declaring her the sweetest baby they'd ever seen. Ben and Jessa even surprised us by showing up unannounced.

When our doctor released us to go home, we nervously buckled Felicity into her car seat. This tiny, helpless infant was now completely our responsibility, with no nurses to rush in when we panicked. We were on our own now, our little family of three.

Jinger

Before we left the hospital, my nurse advised me to take a painkiller for the ride home. I'd only taken ibuprofen since the epidural wore off, and I felt comfortable, but given the two-and-a-half-hour drive ahead, my nurse thought I should try something stronger. Big mistake. Within fifteen minutes, I was dizzy and nauseated. I pulled myself together to smile for a photo with Felicity in her car seat, but as soon as I climbed in the car, I had to lie down in the backseat.

Jeremy drove with my mom in the front seat of our car, which was outfitted with GoPro cameras to capture the ride home for the show. I imagined those cameras recording me losing my hospital lunch all over the backseat. I couldn't even eat when Jeremy stopped at a little popsicle shop for a treat. "I think we ought to turn those cameras off," I finally spoke up. "This is so bad."

Thankfully, the nausea wore off by the time we pulled in our driveway and unloaded the car. We opened the front door of our house and I breathed in deeply, feeling immediately relaxed. When we'd left this house a few days before, Felicity hadn't been born yet. Now here she was, sleeping soundly in her car seat, her chubby cheeks and adorable baby noises melting my heart every time I looked at her. Being home with my daughter was the most amazing feeling.

My mom planned to stay with us for the next two weeks. Every day, she fixed meals for us, made sure I was eating and drinking enough, and took shifts bouncing Felicity for hours so Jeremy and I could get some sleep. I rested whenever I could as my body adjusted to sleeping in such small stretches, and Jeremy or my mom brought me Felicity every few hours for feedings.

From the beginning, I knew Jeremy and I were a team. He was quick to take Felicity when she was upset or needed a diaper change. When I got up at night to feed her, he brought me water or a snack. This was a hard season, but we knew we could manage as long as we walked through it together.

I expected Felicity's newborn days to include a good amount of crying. That's what babies do, after all. I was used to crying babies from living with my siblings, and my mom had experienced everything under the sun. But after a few days passed, I noticed the crying only stopped when Felicity fell asleep. If she was awake, she didn't just cry. She screamed. This was nothing like my experience as a big sister helping my mom. Now, as the mom myself, completely exhausted and responsible twenty-four hours a day for this little life, reality had set in.

I walked through my days in a sleepless fog, crying as Felicity cried, desperate to fix whatever was bothering my daughter. We tried bouncing and shushing. We massaged her belly and pumped her legs. We heated up little packs of oatmeal and wrapped them in a towel before we laid them on her to soothe her tummy. One night, we strapped our screaming daughter in her car seat and drove in the dark, hoping the motion of the car would lull her to sleep. When it didn't, we stopped at the nearest Walgreens, where Jeremy bought about every infant gas remedy on the market.

I grew more and more despondent as each method we tried eventually failed. My baby was crying in pain and I couldn't solve it. I thought of my own mother, who'd experienced the newborn stage nineteen times. *How in the world did she do this?* I thought. Luckily, I had a wealth of knowledge at my fingertips. I had my mom, Jeremy's mom, and my sisters who were just a phone call away.

My diet turned out to be the problem. After getting some advice from my sisters, I gave up all dairy and even several vegetables that were said to cause gas. Sometimes it seemed like I couldn't eat anything at all, and at times, I wasn't sure if it was even helping. Then, when Felicity was about a month old, the clouds lifted. The screaming, red-faced infant I was used to was suddenly content and calm. Felicity's waking hours were no longer filled with crying. I felt like a whole new person—still sleep deprived, but no longer desperate.

Jeremy

I had to admit that I enjoyed the nights I stayed up until 2:00 a.m. holding Felicity. I held her on the couch, watching the *Planet Earth* series on Netflix, willing myself to stay awake. All I could think about were the warnings I'd heard about nodding off and dropping an infant. *Don't fall asleep, don't fall asleep*, I told myself.

More than once, after laying Felicity in her bassinet and going to bed, I woke up completely delirious, freaking out that I'd lost the baby. "Where's

Felicity?" I shouted as I checked the bed and the floor. "Where's Felicity?"

"Shhh." Jinger sat up and rubbed her eyes sleepily. "She's in her bassinet, babe. Don't wake her up."

There were plenty of days when I didn't feel like being patient, when it would have been easier to snap at my wife or yell, "Get it yourself!" when she asked for a glass of water. I'd heard from fellow parents that it was normal to fight and yell while stuck in the throes of sleepless nights and exhausting days.

But Jinger and I decided that the love of Christ, not our circumstances, should control us. We might be tired, and our defenses might be weary, but we knew if we depended on the Holy Spirit even in a trial, we could still experience the fruits described in Galatians 5:22-23—love, joy, peace, patience, kindness, goodness, faithfulness, gentleness, and self-control. The Bible doesn't say that we should have patience when everything is smooth sailing, but when you're sleep deprived you're allowed to have anger and bitterness. Those fruits are available all the time, in any situation.

At the same time, the Bible also doesn't say we can earn the fruits of the Spirit by trying harder. It's not about willpower or your personality. The only way the fruit of the Spirit is produced is by walking with the Spirit. We had to abide with the Lord and be totally dependent on Him.

As new parents, abiding with the Lord looked different than it once had. We couldn't spend hours reading the Bible and praying as we once had. But communing with the Lord isn't a box to check off. It's meant to be life giving, not burdensome. If I couldn't have a formal time of devotions with the Lord, I knew God wasn't looking down on me, shaking his head in disappointment. My prayer life shifted to short, more frequent prayers throughout the day. *Lord, give me strength*, I prayed as I woke from a particularly difficult night. *Lord, direct me*, I prayed when faced with a decision.

Any time I sensed tension creeping into my conversations with Jinger, I stopped and asked myself, *What's going on here? Why am I feeling impatient?* The answer was usually obvious. I wasn't loving her as Christ loved me. The equation is quite simple: the more I love Christ, the more I will love those around me.

Jinger

As a new mom, I frequently battled guilt. I'd enjoyed spending time in the Bible since I developed a hunger for it at fourteen. Now, I was so exhausted that if I had a free moment, all I wanted to do was sleep. *I shouldn't be taking a nap*, a voice nagged at me. *I should be reading the Bible.* I missed my concentrated times of prayer, when I could be with the Lord and come to Him with all of my concerns. I was used to focusing my heart on Christ in a certain way, and at this point, that wasn't possible. Sometimes I felt like I was failing, that I wasn't doing it right, and that if I tried harder, I could do it all.

In those moments, Jeremy was such a strong encouragement to me. He prayed with me, read me devotions or passages from Scripture, and took Felicity on walks so I could read the Bible or even sleep. "It's really OK to take a nap," he told me. "There's nothing to feel guilty about."

I was reminded that God isn't a taskmaster who makes demands of us and is angry when we fall short. God delights in spending time with us and doesn't want that time to be a drudgery. I learned that I could delight in the Lord simply by cuddling my baby, folding laundry, making dinner, or doing any of the tasks I normally would do as a wife and mother. We're called to abide in Christ wherever we are, even if abiding looks different from how it used to. I could be completely worn out from a night up with a teething infant and still have joy if I was abiding.

Jeremy and I certainly had disagreements. There were times I might snap at Jeremy or be short with him. But as we walked in the Spirit, we refused to let anger control us. Our home was still filled with peace, not because we're great people, but because Christ controlled us. We also knew that if we messed up, there was forgiveness. Life as a family of three was beautiful. It was difficult, but even with the night awakenings and dirty diapers, by God's grace, it was beautiful.

Chapter Sixteen

California, Here We Come

Jeremy

"Jeremy, you need to come to The Master's Seminary."

My friend Austin Duncan's words came out of nowhere. Jinger and I were visiting California again when Austin, a professor at The Master's Seminary and pastor at Grace Community Church, invited us for lunch. The conversation flowed easily as we sat with Austin and his wife for hours. We weren't talking about anything even related to seminary when Austin blurted out that sentence.

Austin leaned back in a wicker chair on his back porch. "I know you can't leave Laredo, but we'll let you do it online. We'll create the program and you'll be our guinea pig."

I laughed it off. Austin's known for being a funny guy, so I figured this was a joke.

"Austin, you better be careful what you say," his wife said.

Austin shook his head. "No, no, no. I got it."

His words were still in my head long after we headed to our hotel. Was

Austin serious? Was online seminary really possible? And, more important could I handle it while pastoring full time?

It wasn't that I'd never considered seminary. I enjoyed studying and thought a more advanced degree might be helpful, but it wasn't absolutely necessary. I firmly believe if a man is called by God to be a pastor, the church under him will grow as long as he teaches the Word of God faithfully. Besides, the preacher Charles Spurgeon didn't attend seminary, and he essentially flipped the world upside down. Even so, if I had the opportunity to go, why wouldn't I take it? I never thought it was possible in Laredo, but if Austin was serious about an online program, I needed to give it some thought.

I called Austin the next day. "Hey, before I start praying about seminary, were you serious last night?"

I could practically hear him nodding through the phone. "I've already talked to some people," he said confidently. "Things are in motion. I'll get back to you later this week."

By that fall, I had a stack of textbooks on my desk for three introductory-level courses. I had weekly reading assignments and papers to submit, and every Tuesday, I logged in to watch the prerecorded lectures. Each time, I was blown away by the ocean of understanding these professors opened up to me. Passage by passage, they unveiled the riches and treasures of God's Word, with the thread of God's redemptive purpose woven throughout the Bible from start to finish. It's astonishing how a volume of sixty-six books written by more than forty authors over a two-thousand-year period could be so cohesive.

But it was a heavy load. My pastoral duties hadn't diminished. If anything, they'd increased as my church grew. I had a wife, and now I was also a father. I had no idea how I could do it all and do it well.

Jinger

Hardly a week went by without Jeremy looking at me with exhaustion in his eyes and sighing deeply. "Jinger, if I make it to Sunday afternoon, just remind me that I did it. I made it."

I gave him my most encouraging smile. "You've got this, babe. I'm praying for you."

Jeremy hardly had time to sit and rest now that he'd added seminary to his plate. Still, he went out of his way to make our family his first priority, spending evenings with Felicity and me even if it meant he had to stay up late to finish studying. Sometimes, I sat in his office to be near him as he studied. I scrolled through Instagram or read a good book, trying my best to stay quiet and not distract him.

On his own, Jeremy could go days on end without a meal or a sip of water. I saw firsthand how zapped he felt after preaching Sunday mornings without enough fluids in his system. Once, when I flew to Arkansas to visit my family, I called on Friday, which is typically his big study day.

"What have you eaten today?" I asked, knowing his history.

"Uh…" Jeremy paused a moment before he admitted, "a pack of Skittles and a Clif Bar."

"Babe!" I imagined my husband hunched over his computer, too busy to notice his stomach growling. "You have to eat. Promise me you're going to eat."

Jeremy agreed to go to a friend's house for dinner that night. While he's more than capable of fixing himself something to eat, I knew from experience that he gets so focused on the task at hand that he doesn't think about food. I never understood how he could do that. I'm pretty sure my blood sugar would take a nosedive and I'd pass out if I only ate Skittles all day long.

As long as I was home, I made it my mission to keep Jeremy fed and hydrated. I couldn't study for his tests and write his papers, but I could bring him honey lattes and glasses of ice water. It wasn't much, but it was something. Just as Jeremy used to bring me water and snacks while I nursed Felicity, this was a simple way for us to serve each other.

My favorite moments came when Jeremy learned something interesting in a class or a verse of Scripture came to life to him in a new way. We sat together on the couch for hours, dialoguing back and forth and digging into theology, and sometimes I even watched his lectures. I was as fascinated by his classes as he was and looked forward to those discussions. I felt included, involved in a piece of his life that I could easily have been left out of.

I could see the toll his double workload took on him. Every once in a while, I had a fleeting thought about how much easier it would be if Jeremy could attend seminary in person, and if he could concentrate on nothing but his studies. My mind drifted to our trips to California, to my walks with my friends and the other ladies I'd met, how it felt like we already fit in there even though we had only visited sporadically. I thought of all the godly men pouring into Jeremy from a distance, and how good it would be for him to be mentored after all these years of pouring himself out for others. I didn't want to leave Laredo. I loved our ministry there and could see us staying until we retired. But I felt something tugging at my heart, even though I didn't want to admit it.

As months went by, Jeremy got calls here and there from other ministry opportunities around the country. We prayed about them, but nothing seemed right. We were called to Laredo, Jeremy told them each time.

When Jeremy told me about another opportunity he'd been offered one night, I figured he would have the same response.

"I really don't feel like that's where the Lord is leading us right now," he said. His voice was absent, as if he was thinking about something else. "But," he continued, "I *am* feeling pressed about Los Angeles."

"Yeah, me too." My eyes filled with tears the moment those words flew out of my mouth. *Wait, what? Did I just say that?* California had been on my heart, but as long as I never said the words out loud, I didn't have to take it seriously. Now, it wasn't only me. Jeremy felt pressed too. Without us realizing it, the Lord had been working all along.

This is crazy, I thought. *How can we leave Laredo? Our friends are here. We can't leave our ministry. We bought a house! Our hearts are in this town. We can't move.*

As I looked into Jeremy's eyes, I knew he was serious. "I don't know, Jer." I leaned into his chest, trying to make sense of my swirling thoughts. "Is this good? Should we even pray about it? Or are we thinking about something that we shouldn't?"

We prayed together in the quiet of our living room, crying out to the Lord and asking him for guidance. "Show us your will, God," we prayed. "Help us to recognize your providences and follow your lead."

Jeremy

In the coming days, I met with a few men from the Laredo church and sought their advice. They didn't give me a definitive answer but gave me a few options to consider, like doing school online and visiting LA once a quarter, or even spending a semester in LA before returning to Laredo.

"Guys, you've brought up some good points," I told them. "Let me pray about this and get back to you."

God, I can't move my family to California and leave my church on a "maybe," I prayed. *There's too much at stake. I need a clear yes or no.*

I scheduled a call that Friday with the seminary's vice president of students. For the next five days, I fasted as I sought the Lord. I needed this meeting to give me clarity and steer me in the right direction.

The vice president was frank with me when I picked up the phone for our meeting.

"Jeremy, look," he said. "You can do seminary online. But the reality is, your experience is going to be like the diet soda version. It's going to be like training to become a doctor by watching YouTube rather than being in the hospital."

By the time I hung up, my uncertainty was gone. "I have so much peace about going," I said to Jinger as we sat together on the couch.

She looked up at me, her eyes sad but resolute. "Yeah, me too. It's going to be hard, but it's so clear."

If Jinger and I had been dissatisfied in Laredo and actively looking for a way out, I'd be skeptical of our motives. But we were completely happy in Laredo. As we asked the Lord to show us his will, it turned out all we needed to do was take a step back and open our eyes. God had been lining up our lives to move to California since the day we first stepped on the Grace Community Church campus. We weren't even supposed to be in California on our honeymoon in the first place, and we had stumbled upon the church as we searched for a bookstore, but person after person welcomed us and ministered to us. I didn't ask to sit down with Pastor John for hours, or to be invited back to campus multiple times, or to be asked to be the guinea pig for The Master's Seminary's online program. It was all God.

As we looked at these providences from a distance, we realized God hadn't just cracked open the door. He'd kicked it open so hard it fell off the hinges. Jinger and I were left standing on the other side, looking through the opening and thinking, *I guess he wants us to walk through this door*. When I asked myself if I'd be better suited to serve in ministry if I had a seminary degree, the answer was unequivocally yes. I had the opportunity to attend one of the best seminaries and learn from men who led how I wanted to lead. I had the desire to study. And as a young couple with a baby, we could move across the country and adjust relatively quickly.

Second only to the Lord's leading was the fact that Jinger was on board. Jinger and I are a team. While we believe that God calls husbands to lead their households, we also believe that a good leader isn't a dictator. A team like that will never succeed. I would never force my wife to do something that she disagreed with. The fact that she was immediately on the same page was evidence that God was leading us.

A move to LA was intimidating. We knew the city was expensive, with world-famous traffic and a housing market that's notoriously high priced. But I wasn't worried. "If God is leading us there, He'll provide," I told Jinger. "He'll provide a job. He'll provide housing. We don't need to worry."

That February 2019, we watched in awe as God put the remaining pieces of the puzzle together. "Get on out here!" our friends in California said when we announced we were coming. "It's about time!" Our friends sprang into action right away to help. They offered me a job at Grace Community Church's conference department, and they introduced me to a kind, servant-hearted couple who happened to own apartments and rental properties throughout the city. The two of them showed us around and helped us choose a house close to my job. I could make it home for dinner every night without fighting the infamous LA traffic. I could even stop at home for lunch to spend time with Jinger and Felicity. It was perfect.

When we told our parents the news, no one was surprised. Both Jinger's parents and my mom and dad barely even flinched. "Oh, yeah, we saw this coming," they said.

"What!" I said, my jaw dropping. We'd thought our parents would be shocked we'd even consider LA. Jinger and I looked at each other incredulously. "How? *We* didn't see it coming!"

All that was left was the hardest part—telling our church. I didn't want any members to hear the news from someone other than me. For one week, I spent nearly every hour of every day meeting one-on-one with each church member.

I was nervous as I sat down at a restaurant across from a young guy named Ben to break the news. He was the first person I told, and I had no idea how to get the words out.

After we made small talk for a while, I took a deep breath and cleared my throat. "Hey, Ben, there's something I need to tell you."

Ben perked up and looked at me. "Yeah, what's up?"

His enthusiastic tone broke my heart. *I need to soften the blow here somehow.* "I need to tell you, it's not good news."

"OK." Ben frowned.

"It's about me and Jinger." Right away I froze. *Oh my, that sounds terrible!* I backtracked. "Well, it's not that bad. Nothing's wrong with me and Jinger. Our relationship's great." I practically stuttered as I fumbled for words.

Ben laughed and leaned forward, his face reassuring. "Jeremy, as long as you don't tell me you're leaving, everything's fine."

His words were like a punch in the gut. I could feel my face turning red as I stammered, "Well, actually, that's what's happening." I could tell from the look on Ben's face that he was crushed.

When we finally finished our conversation, Ben offered me a piece of advice. "Jeremy, when you tell other people, you need to lead into it a little better. Let them see it coming."

Ben was right. This was practically like a breakup. I needed to find a way to let everyone down easy.

That week was brutal. I spent my days in meeting after meeting, sometimes as many as six in a day, most of them lasting an hour and a half. I took Ben's advice and started my conversations reminding them that I was an online student at The Master's Seminary, and that Jinger and I had visited California several times. While everybody received the news well and they all seemed happy for us, it was still heartbreaking. That's the nature of leaving a ministry you've poured your heart and soul into, a ministry where you planned to stay forever. Sometimes I was tempted to throw up my hands and shout, "Never mind!" How could I leave when I was hurting so many people? In those moments I remembered my mom's words so long ago: "Don't doubt in the dark what God has shown you in the light." This was God's will. I knew it and Jinger knew it. We were walking forward, no matter how difficult it was in the moment.

Jinger

When we told the church and the clouds of sadness cleared, I finally allowed myself to feel excited. I'd always loved the city, and the idea that I would actually live in one of the biggest cities in the country was almost more than I could fathom. I thought of the beaches, the mountains, the museums, the shops, the restaurants with every kind of cuisine you could imagine. There was so much variety, so much hustle and bustle. I couldn't wait to live there. *Man, we're going to have so much fun on our days off,* I thought.

While I knew LA was a very secular city, I wasn't concerned. Jeremy and I both agree that it doesn't matter whether you live in Los Angeles, Texas, or Arkansas. The problem of sin isn't found in a geographical location. The problem of sin is in the heart. That's how Grace Community Church had thrived with such a beautiful ministry in a city known for movies and celebrities.

I was a little nervous about selling our house, especially when we'd barely owned it for a year. But I staged the house as best I could, and we hired a photographer from church to take professional, wide-angle photos. I couldn't believe it when we had an offer within twenty-four hours of listing our house.

We scheduled our move in June, about three months after we announced our plans to the church. It seemed so far away at the time, but the weeks flew by faster than I could keep track. Before I knew it, I was sitting in church with tears in my eyes as Jeremy preached his last sermon.

It had been a whirlwind of a week. After closing on our house on a Thursday, Jeremy and I packed every last pot, pan, and baby toy in boxes. I was too distracted to label them properly. I was amazed at how much more stuff we'd collected since we'd moved from our apartment into this house. A few church members helped us load our boxes into a truck that movers hauled to California, along with one of our cars. Then, we scrubbed every inch of the house until it was sparkling for the new owners. Jeremy and I were so exhausted we could barely stand. It took a trip out for ice cream to give us the energy we needed to finish mopping the floors.

Some friends let us stay at their house until Monday, when we planned to drive west. I felt emotional and weepy leading up to Jeremy's final sermon, but once he prayed over the congregation one last time, I felt closure. We had served our calling in Laredo. We were faithful. I could fully allow myself to look forward to the adventure ahead.

Jeremy

I felt a strange sense of relief as I finished my last sermon. It was the close of a chapter, and the start of a brand-new one. Jinger and I were about to embark on an adventure together.

With permission from our host, we invited a few friends from church over that afternoon for one final get-together. Jinger had regularly held game nights with church singles for months, and we decided to have one more.

We were deep in the middle of Codenames when Jinger's phone rang. "It's my mom," she said. "I'll just be a second."

I didn't pay much attention as she walked to the next room to answer her phone. My mind was on the game until I heard her shout, "No!"

I looked up in time to see her drop to her knees, weeping.

I rushed over to hold her as she fell to pieces on the floor. I didn't say a word, but I knew someone had died. I just didn't know who.

Chapter Seventeen

His Joy Comes in the Morning

Jinger

My hand shook as I held my phone to my face. My legs had already given way beneath me, and I could feel the carpet of my friend's living room digging into my knees. I heard my mom's words, but they didn't make sense. They couldn't be true. There had to be some mistake.

Grandma Duggar, a constant figure in my life, the woman who taught me to sew on buttons, my shopping buddy and confidante, had died. She'd had a couple strokes recently, and I made a special trip to Arkansas three months earlier so she could spend time with Felicity. But she hadn't died of natural causes or passed away peacefully in her sleep. Grandma Duggar drowned in her backyard pool.

The thought of my beloved grandma dying in such a tragic way made me sick. I couldn't even speak the words as Jeremy consoled me and asked what had happened.

"I'm so sorry I had to tell you this way," Mom said over and over on the phone. "I'm just so sorry."

Growing up, Grandma Duggar had been over at our house practically twenty-four hours a day, seven days a week. Mom's mother had died right after she had Jill, and ever since, Grandma had been there for my mom. The two of them grew close and had such a sweet bond. Grandma ran errands for us, picked up our mail, and watched us kids so Mom and Dad could have date nights. She and Grandpa were always supportive and willing to help out. When Grandpa got cancer, they moved in with us so we could help. I watched her tirelessly care for him and sit by his bedside every single day.

Grandma was always up for a trip to Braum's for ice cream, or to McDonald's for a fish sandwich. She took Jessa and me shopping and taught us the best places to find cute used clothes. Grandma never met a stain she couldn't get out, and she taught me everything she knew. She and I were close and spent quite a bit of time together. Losing her hurt so much I could physically feel it.

Jeremy held me on the couch as I sobbed. Our friends respectfully retreated to another room to give us some privacy. I finally managed to tell Jeremy what had happened, and we cried together for my grandma, for the gaping hole she would leave behind in our family.

"Grandma Duggar loved God," Jeremy whispered, stroking my back. "She's with the Lord now. She's being ushered into glory. That's infinitely better than being here."

Those words weren't a flat platitude or a cliché. They were filled with hope. As soon as Jeremy said them, I remembered that her death was not an end. As much as I would miss her, how could I wish she were here instead of with God? She wasn't only in a better place—she was in the arms of her savior, the place she'd waited faithfully for all her life. I felt my sobs slow down and my body relax. The steady stream of tears eventually dried.

Our friends came back in the room and prayed with us. "I totally understand if you need us to leave," one of our friends said.

Surprisingly, that was the last thing I wanted. I didn't want to curl up in a ball and lie on my bed in the dark. I was sad, but I wasn't destroyed. In that moment, being with people I loved was the best thing for me.

"No," I said with a peace I didn't know I could have. "I'm OK. I'm sad, but I'm OK."

We ended up meeting several friends at our old favorite restaurant, Taquitos Ravi. As we laughed and talked, I still felt the ache of sadness. My eyes still filled with tears any time I thought of her. But surrounded by my friends, I still had joy. I would see my grandma again.

Jeremy

I was amazed at how quickly Jinger was consoled and calmed after hearing the horrific news of her grandmother's death. No one would have blamed her if she'd fallen apart. Instead, the knowledge that her grandmother was with the Lord soothed her spirit. It was a testament to the joy of the Lord, available to us in any circumstance, even in the hour of heartbreak and tragedy.

There was no question that we had to leave for Arkansas the next day. Our move to California had to wait. Our place was with Jinger's family, and at the service celebrating her grandmother's life. We left early the next morning for Springdale. As soon as we arrived at the Big House, I could tell the weight of Jinger's loss had fully sunk in. My heart broke for her as she and her mom held each other, weeping. I felt a lump in my throat as I saw Mr. and Mrs. Duggar's red-rimmed eyes. They looked exhausted, worn out from crying. The house felt strangely empty, even though it was still filled to bursting with Jinger's siblings. Grandma Duggar's presence, which had always loomed large, was gone, and you could feel it.

I was grateful Jinger could be there to comfort her family, help Mrs. Duggar with funeral arrangements, and remember her grandmother at a private family viewing. She leaned into me with tears in her eyes as a few of her brothers and sisters shared their memories of their grandma.

The day of her funeral, I put on a black suit, Jinger a black dress. I held her hand as we walked into First Baptist Church in Springdale. At least two thousand people filled the seats, their eyes on us as Jinger clung to me, already in tears. Sitting in the service was surreal. The casket was surrounded by brightly colored floral arrangements. It felt final, and this was really the moment we said goodbye to Grandma Duggar. I could tell from the look on Jinger's face that she was flooded with memories—memories that one day would comfort her but today brought grief. My heart broke for her as we walked to the casket for one last goodbye, Jinger's body shaking as she wept.

It was raining as we left the church for the cemetery. People huddled under the awning that covered the freshly dug grave and crowded under umbrellas as Jinger's brothers carried in the casket. I was humbled and honored when Jinger's family asked me to preach the graveside service. I felt a deep sense of responsibility as I opened my Bible to John 20 and the account of Christ's resurrection. This gospel account is different from the others, for in this one, we read of Mary Magdalene encountering her risen Savior. Initially, she mistook him for the gardener, until he called her name, "Mary!" In that instant, Mary recognized her savior and exclaimed, "Rabboni!" which means teacher or master. As I read the text, I spoke of the power Christ has over death, not only for Himself but also for all who put their faith in Him. But I also noticed a poignant parallel—*Grandma Duggar's name was Mary*, I thought. *The parallel is incredible.*

Before Jinger's family and friends, I shared that death is an enemy, but it's an enemy that Jesus already conquered when He was crucified and rose from the grave. "Even though we stand here looking into the grave of Grandma Duggar, because the grave could not hold Jesus Christ, it will not hold her," I said.

"Last Sunday, over a week ago, she heard that same sweet sound uttered from the mouth of Christ: 'Mary!' And she was embraced by her Rabboni, never to leave his perfect presence again."

I saw Jinger's family's faces light up as they connected their grandma's name to the passage I'd referenced. While we wept for the loss of a beloved woman, for the person whose presence we would deeply miss, we weren't in despair. The graveside was not dark or bleak. Even as we mourned, there was hope.

Jinger

I felt relieved as we returned to my family's house for a meal after the service. The heavy burden I'd carried since the moment I learned of Grandma Duggar's death was gone. As hard as the service was, it was sweet and God-glorifying. It gave me a sense of closure I didn't know I needed. I felt lighter and more relaxed as my family and I shared memories and laughed together over stories of Grandma's bargain shopping and her penchant for calling everybody to warn them of a tornado. In my family's living room, I was so grateful for the time I'd had with my grandma, and for the opportunity to see her a few months before she passed.

While we didn't plan it this way, our trip to Arkansas also gave me a chance to say goodbye to my parents and siblings before we headed west. We had a few days to enjoy family time and catch up with one another. My heart was heavy as I hugged Mom and Dad goodbye and strapped Felicity in her car seat. While I'd lived away from them for some time now, California was much farther than Laredo. Still, I knew we were only a plane ride away. "We'll come visit soon," Mom and Dad assured me.

The road ahead of us was long—more than 1,500 miles, to be precise. When you take a road trip with a baby, you can't wing it. You have to make a plan. Jeremy and I decided to stretch the trip over five days, stopping a couple times each day for lunch and to visit sights, like the Cadillac Ranch in Texas. Felicity was a true road trip champion. She fell asleep as soon as we started the car in the morning, played during our stops, and went right back to sleep in the afternoon. Jeremy and I talked for hours as we drove through Oklahoma, Texas, New Mexico, and Arizona. Waves of sadness would hit me now and then, but I was comforted by remembering Jeremy's words. Grandma was with her Rabboni now.

As we crossed the California border, I felt a jittery sense of excitement. *Wow*, I thought. *This is our home.* The church we'd felt drawn toward but thought we'd never be part of was now going to be our church. I was filled with anticipation.

The first few days were a busy haze of unpacking and getting used to our new surroundings. The house we'd rented came fully furnished, so we stored away all our furniture and anything else we didn't need yet. I looked around at the spacious, open-concept two-story house with a fenced backyard that even had an orange tree. Even on a summer day, it wasn't nearly as hot as Laredo, where summers are so steamy that all you want to do is sit in the air-conditioning. I smiled as it finally sank in that this was where we lived. The Lord had provided so graciously.

Since Jeremy's classes hadn't started yet, we had time to relax and explore our new home. We cheered for the home team at an LA Galaxy game, listened to a symphony orchestra at Mozart under the Stars at the Hollywood Bowl, and took a food crawl through the city, eating as much good food and drinking as much coffee as our bodies could handle.

Every day there was something new to experience, and now that Jeremy wasn't juggling pastoring and seminary, he was actually free to enjoy it with Felicity and me. It felt like a mini vacation, and we loved taking it all in. I had to remind myself that we didn't need to cram every second of every day with activity, that we had all the time in the world to experience our new city. We did hit one bump in the road—an earthquake that shook our home for forty-two seconds and left Jeremy with a splitting headache. I'd experienced tornadoes and severe storms, but this was a different level. I felt vulnerable and creeped out. At first, I declared that I was ready to move home, but soon, I was able to laugh it off. One little earthquake wasn't enough to derail God's plan for us.

I expected to feel out of place when we first moved to LA, and I thought that it would take quite some time before it really felt like home. Thanks to the friends and church waiting for us here, that wasn't the case. Our friendships only deepened now that we lived here full time, and Jeremy and I quickly found ourselves with a close-knit group of friends. We didn't feel lost in a foreign land. We felt like we belonged.

Jeremy

After months of only watching classes on a screen, I was eager to jump into my classes in person and soak in the wisdom of my professors. I loved interacting with my fellow students and engaging in class discussions. I loved having the opportunity to ask a professor questions during office hours and getting lunch with colleagues. It was a joy to constantly rub shoulders with other guys devoted to ministry. While the workload was intense, and I still had tests to take and papers to write, it was nothing compared to the pressure of taking classes while also caring for the souls of my congregation. I knew that this season was unique and temporary, and I was determined to enjoy every second of it.

Our new home had plenty of space for hosting, and Jinger and I filled our home as often as we could with LA friends and visitors from out of town. We loved taking long walks with Felicity and visiting the church campus playground, watching Felicity play and making sure she didn't get too close to the edge of a slide. By now, Felicity was one year old, and she was blossoming. My favorite moments came at the end of the day, when Felicity greeted me at the door, and we ran through the house together. Her sweet laughter melted my heart every time.

It didn't take a keen observer to notice Felicity was a people person by nature. She was Little Miss Social. Her face lit up in a smile any time she was around babies and other kids, and she never met an adult she didn't like. Once, as we waited in line for hot chicken from Howlin' Ray's, Felicity walked right up to a woman passing us and grabbed her hand. She was content as could be holding this woman's hand, who looked back at us with a baffled smile. Felicity rocks her dolls to sleep and will gingerly cradle anything from her snack to her shoes, hushing and shushing it like she sees her mommy and daddy do. *This girl isn't meant to be alone*, I thought. *She's made to be a big sister.*

Jinger and I had talked about wanting our kids to be about two years apart, but we weren't in a rush. We had moved across the country and been through so much change, and we didn't have a specific time line in mind. After a couple months in LA, we decided the time was right. We were ready for another baby.

When Jinger felt a little off that November, a pregnancy test confirmed her suspicions. Another baby was on the way. I grinned as I tenderly placed my hand on Jinger's belly, in awe of the life growing inside her. I wondered what this little one would be like. Would it be a boy or a girl? Would they be like Felicity or totally different? I pictured Felicity stroking her new sibling's soft, downy hair, and her squeals of excitement as she carefully held the baby for the first time. Those moments would be so sweet, so special.

We told our families we were expecting right before Thanksgiving. We set up our Christmas tree, a live one we cut down ourselves, and FaceTimed with my family after trimming it with lights and ornaments. My mom and dad shouted with excitement when they noticed the ornament strategically hung at the front, with "Baby Due Summer 2020" printed in bold letters. For Jinger's family, we decided to announce our good news during a family gingerbread house competition. The Duggars have a family night most Monday evenings, and that week, each family decorated a gingerbread house. Whoever created the best gingerbread house would be crowned the winner. We built one too, complete with a little ginger family, and FaceTimed with the family to show off our handiwork. It took them at least three minutes to notice the pregnant belly on the gingerbread Jinger. The film crew captured every squeal of excitement as everyone put two and two together and realized we were having a baby. Those evenings were beautiful, a time of celebrating with our families and looking toward the future with expectation.

Jinger

Not long after the gingerbread competition, I felt the first cramp. The ache was persistent, impossible to ignore. *Maybe I need to rest*, I told myself. *Maybe I overdid it today.* I lay down on the couch and tried to relax. Cramping was normal, right? I told myself everything was OK, that I'd feel better in a few hours. By the time I went to bed, I only felt worse.

The cramping shook me from my sleep in the middle of the night. This wasn't an ache anymore. The pain was intense now, and I knew I couldn't go back to sleep. A cold fear overwhelmed me, a fear I didn't want to put into words. *Something's not right*, I thought. *Something is wrong with the baby.*

The sun hadn't yet lit the sky that morning when I rushed to the bathroom. Part of me still clung to the hope that my cramping was one of those aches and pains of pregnancy. But when I looked down and saw the toilet bowl full of blood, I knew.

I sat there in shock. I'd heard of people having miscarriages. My mom and sisters-in-law had experienced that tragedy, but naively, I never thought it would happen to me. How could this be real? Since the day I'd seen the positive pregnancy test, I had been so excited about Felicity having a sibling. I dreamed of nursing my baby as Felicity cuddled beside us, of pushing them around the neighborhood in a double stroller, of gathering both kids on my lap as I read them a story. And just like that, those dreams were gone. I sat on the cold tile of the bathroom and hugged my knees to my chest, sobbing for the baby I never knew, the sibling Felicity wouldn't have. I wanted that baby so badly, but that wasn't enough to save it. *God, this is so painful*, I wept. *I didn't think this would happen. But I know you're good. I know you're in control.* That prayer gave me the strength to stand up again.

I crept back into the bedroom and tapped Jeremy's shoulder. "I think we've lost the baby," I whispered. The pain I saw flash across his face was more than I could take.

Jeremy stood to his feet and pulled me into his chest. I could feel him crying too, even though I couldn't see his face. "The Lord gives, and the Lord takes away," he said hoarsely. "Blessed be the name of the Lord."

I knew he was quoting a passage from the book of Job. I thought of Job as we lay together on the bed, the early morning sun streaking through the window. Job was a man who loved the Lord, and he lost everything—his children, his wealth, his health—all in one day. And yet, in the book of James, Job's story is summarized in verse 11 as, "You have heard of the steadfastness of Job, and you have seen the purpose of the Lord, how the Lord is compassionate and merciful." *God hasn't changed*, I thought. *He's still full of compassion and mercy. I believe He is who He says*

He is, even in my pain. I felt peace, even as I felt a grief deeper than I'd ever experienced. I didn't understand why I'd lost this baby, but I had hope in the fact that Jeremy and I wouldn't walk through this alone. The Lord was with us. He wouldn't leave us. He wouldn't forsake us. He is who He has always been.

Jeremy

Jinger's mom encouraged us to get to a doctor right away, in case there was a chance the baby could be saved. Jinger's midwife in Texas connected her to a birth center in Los Angeles that could see us right away. Providentially, my sister, Valerie, was visiting at the time and could watch Felicity for us.

My heart pounded as the ultrasound technician moved the probe around Jinger's belly, looking for a heartbeat. She looked and looked, pausing and looking concerned before looking some more. Deep down I knew. The ultrasound shouldn't take this long. Not if everything was normal. Not if this bleeding was nothing but a scare.

"I'm so sorry," she finally said. "There's no heartbeat."

Her words were crushing. I'd known the baby was most likely gone, but part of me was still holding on to hope that maybe there was a chance. Jinger and I held each other there in the exam room, crying for our baby who was now with its Maker.

The days that followed were dark. We spent most of them on the couch, crying and comforting each other. Valerie was incredible and took care of us so well. She filled our bare fridge with groceries, brought Jinger flowers, cooked for us, and played with Felicity as we came to grips with our grief.

On the couch with Jinger, I thought of the timing of our loss, the sad irony that we lost our baby the same weekend we told our entire family.

We had just celebrated with everyone and basked in the joy of their excitement. Why, after we'd told everyone? Why, when our announcement was filmed for the show? We had loved that child since the moment we knew it existed. And now it was gone?

This was the greatest trial we'd walked through together. Yet the Bible tells us that trials are going to come. It's not a matter of if, but when. It's easy to trust God when everything is rosy, your family is healthy, your career is going well, and you have a nice place to live. It's another thing altogether when the rug is pulled out from under you without warning. If God is good in times of prosperity, then I knew without a doubt that he was good in my darkest days too. And that knowledge gave us hope. We don't have to despair when tragedy strikes. Even in our grief, we knew this trial was refining us, shaping us, making us more like Christ.

As the clouds parted, Jinger and I slowly rose back to the surface. We put one foot in front of the other again, returned to our church activities, resumed life as normal. We hadn't forgotten our loss. We still mourned our baby. But we knew that as hard as this trial was, we would get through it. By walking with the Lord, we would get through it.

Our hope was not in a happy ending. God wasn't good only if he gave us another baby and everything turned out how we wanted. The truth was we didn't know what was coming next. The tragedies and hardships we'd experienced might pale in comparison to what's ahead. Still, we aren't afraid. Just as He always has, the Lord will continue to be faithful and true. He won't fail us. No matter how dark our sorrow, His joy always comes with the morning.

Epilogue

The Hope We Hold

Jeremy

I could hear Felicity and Jinger in the kitchen as I sat upstairs in my office.

"Lissy!" Jinger called. "Let's eat some lunch!"

I smiled at the sound of her voice. I could picture Felicity in her high chair, yogurt smeared around her lips, and Jinger sitting next to her, her belly growing with the baby we were expecting—a new child God had blessed us with after such a tragic loss. *God is so good*, I thought. I stood up to head downstairs and join them when a box caught my eye. My old journals.

Since 2012, I've written detailed journal entries almost daily. I always included the date, time, and where I was when I wrote it, and sometimes I even pasted in a picture or memento. Even if all I had time to write was, "Got lunch with a friend," I tried to write something as often as I could.

My curiosity got the better of me as I reached into the box, pulling out my journal from my days with the New York Red Bulls. Instantly, memories flooded back—the sights, smells, and tastes, how I felt as my pen scribbled across the page. I flipped through one journal, and then another. Before I knew it, I'd completely lost track of time.

A knock on the door frame startled me from my trance. I looked up to see Jinger. "You ready for lunch, babe?"

"You have to look at this." I handed her the journal I'd lost myself in for the last several minutes. "It's just astonishing. I wasn't looking for it at the time, but hope was there all along."

Like a silver thread woven through our story, hope was a part of the very fabric of our lives. It was there when my soccer career was seemingly crumbling almost as quickly as it started. It was there when I was lonely and longed for a wife. It was there when I prayed about Jinger from afar, and when I spent months talking to Mr. Duggar in hopes of getting his permission to pursue her. It was there during that dark week at the conference, when Jinger suddenly had a change of heart. It was there throughout our long-distance relationship, and as we said, "I do." It was there through the heights of our ministry in Laredo, and as we welcomed Felicity into our family. It was there in our sorrow, in Grandma Duggar's tragic death, in the loss of our unborn baby.

In each of those circumstances, in joy and in despair, neither Jinger nor I could control what would happen. The future seemed uncertain and frightening at times. It does even now. After all, there's no shortage of things that can go wrong. I could easily get lost in anxiety and worry. What if we have another miscarriage? What if Jinger gets cancer? What if I get cancer? What if Felicity is in an accident? What if I lose my job?

So many of us are obsessed with tomorrow, scrambling for security, for some semblance of control. We all want reassurance that everything's going to be OK. The reality is, it might not be OK. Horrible tragedies happen every day. If we put our hope in our circumstances, we will be disappointed. Nothing in this world can offer us true hope.

It's only when we fix our eyes on the person and promises of Christ that we have hope. Even if those promises are still unseen, we can walk forward boldly, knowing that they will be fulfilled one day. The Christian can look toward the future with confidence, free of fear. We aren't afraid of tomorrow because we know who holds tomorrow.

When we look at the woman described in Proverbs 31, Scripture tells us she looks at the future and laughs. I love that imagery. Throughout the book of Proverbs, we have a father and mother urging their son to marry Lady Wisdom, not Lady Folly. What is too often viewed as a smattering of sayings is instead a description of both a life of wisdom and a life of folly. Then, in Chapter 31, the final chapter of the book, the woman described is actually the epitome of wisdom, someone we should all aspire to be, not just women. This is a woman who fears the Lord, who serves Him with her life. She doesn't lie awake in her bed at night, worrying about the difficulties that might lie ahead. She looks at the future and says, "Ha! Bring it, tomorrow!" That trust, that peace, is incredible. And any of us can have that same peace. Rich or poor, strong or weak, known or unknown, that hope is available.

When we have that eternal perspective, nothing can crush us. The rest of the world might look at worst-case scenarios, like a terminal cancer diagnosis, with utter despair. To the Christian, death is only the start of eternity. When we're communing with God and enjoying a relationship with Him, physical death only draws us into nearer and sweeter communion with our Lord. While we enjoy this world and the people in it, we know this world is not our home. Death is not a hopeless, inescapable reality. It's an eagerly awaited transition from a temporal existence to eternity.

If we really grasp this hope, our entire perspective is transformed. This hope might not change our circumstances, but it will radically reshape how we view and walk through our circumstances. Anyone who holds on to the eternal promises of God, knowing and understanding who God is, can endure even the most difficult circumstances and trials with joy. Whether we're in the throes of difficulty or on the mountaintop of joy, our hope is unwavering.

God's promises that He will never change, that He will never leave us nor forsake us, have guided Jinger and me every step of the way. Those promises shape every decision we make, every action we take. Those promises are the foundation of our lives.

Jinger

I was amazed at the hope shining through Jeremy's journals. Looking back on my journey, on our journey, I was surprised at every twist and turn, but God wasn't. He was in control, even when I felt out of control.

The reality is, there is no guarantee that our circumstances will get better. But hope in Christ changes how we view and walk through our circumstances. Good times and hard times will come and go, but the promises of God never change. Matthew 11:28 tells us, "Come to me, all who labor and are heavy laden, and I will give you rest" (ESV). So many of us are weary and heavy laden, perhaps now more than ever. And Jesus promises us rest from all of it if we come to Him. The rest Jesus promises is rest for our souls. It's such a sweet promise in a world where millions of people are struggling with depression and anxiety. Other leaders and philosophers offer theories and ways of living, but they can't guarantee this rest.

God does not promise to take away the thing that is making you weary, but He guarantees you peace in the midst of the storm. Life may not be easy. But there's joy. There's peace. There's hope. Philippians 4:4 tells us, "Rejoice in the Lord always; again I will say, rejoice" (ESV). Notice that Paul, the author of Philippians, doesn't say "some of the time" or even "most of the time." He says "always." Honestly, I can't do that. No one can on their own. So why does Paul ask this of us? He goes on to explain. "Do not be anxious about anything," he writes in verse 6, "but in everything by prayer and supplication with thanksgiving let your requests be made known to God" (ESV). We don't have to be anxious because we can take our worries to the Lord in prayer. We can cast our cares upon Him. This way of living will change us in a way the rest of the world can't fathom. Paul says in verse 7, "And the peace of God, which surpasses all understanding, will guard your hearts and your minds in Christ Jesus" (ESV).

This is a supernatural reality of the Christian life. I look back on that day when I clutched the phone, listening to my mother telling me the terrible news of Grandma Duggar's death. Even as my heart was dashed, as I fell to the floor weeping, there was peace. As Jeremy and I sat together on the couch, going through tissue after tissue, unable to move as we mourned the loss of our unborn child, there was still joy. I couldn't explain it at the time, but I had joy knowing that God knew exactly what he was doing. He's a good father. He loves us and cares for us. I knew my little one and my grandma were in the care of my Savior. I can rest in that knowledge. No one would have blamed me if I questioned my faith after those tragedies. Why would I doubt God in the midst of tragedy? It's in those moments that I need Him the most. In times of desperation, anguish, and pain, there is no better place for me than to rest in the arms of the Christ. In my darkest moments, He was there, still faithful, still true.

Jeremy and I aren't special people with perfect temperaments and charmed lives. The lives we lead, the relationship we have, is only possible because of our hope in Christ. And this hope isn't exclusive. It's available to anyone who wants it. Christians who have lost sight of the hope available to them can lay their burdens down to their father in Heaven.

Anyone who doesn't know the Lord is invited into a relationship with Him—"Whoever comes to me I will never cast out" (John 6:37, ESV).

Our hope is found in a daily communion with the Lord. We read our Bibles and pray throughout our days not because we have to, but because it's our lifeline. God's Word is literally our daily bread. If we're not abiding constantly, our old worries and anxieties creep back in. Our sinful natures rear their ugly heads. There are no good works or formulaic prayers that can give you this hope. Nothing but an intimate relationship with the living God through Jesus Christ will bring you these blessings.

Salvation is defined by being in Christ, by unifying the believer with the Savior. Those two words, "in Christ," are peppered throughout the New Testament. When you read those words, the whole New Testament comes alive with realities of what we can have because we're in Christ. We have peace. Joy. Stability. Strength. Blessing. Opportunity. We have everything! This isn't a formula. This is a relationship. You need to be united with Christ. How do you do that? Repent of your sins, put your faith in Him as your Lord and Savior, and He will unite Himself to you and rescue you from your sins. No "ifs." That's a promise.

If you close this book thinking, "Wow, what a nice couple; too bad I can't have a life like theirs," we've failed. It is our goal that you walk away inspired by what the hope of Christ has done for us, and what it can do for you too. The truth is, we're not special. We don't have an extraordinary marriage because we're inherently good people with mild tempers, and we certainly don't have all the answers. Our joy, our peace, our hope, are rooted in the promise of 1 Peter Chapter 1, that in God's great mercy "he has caused us to be born again into a living hope through the resurrection of Jesus Christ from the dead, to an inheritance that is imperishable, undefiled, and unfading" (1 Peter 1:3–4, ESV).

I don't know what the future holds. I don't know where the Lord will take Jeremy and me, or what He will call us to. If the past is any indication, the Lord will write a story for us that I couldn't predict. There will be happiness, and there will certainly be pain. There may be moments I don't know if I can do it, that I wonder if it's more than we can handle. Even so, we will walk forward in confidence. The Lord has always been faithful. He will be again. No matter what awaits us, our hope is in Christ alone.

Acknowledgments

If we're honest, the initial thought of writing this book was a bit daunting. We knew that it would require us to open windows into our world that even the TV cameras never peered into. We'd share dimensions of our journey—like hidden fears and anxious thoughts—that we'd only ever shared with each other. The challenge loomed large, yet we knew we had a story of hope that needed to be told. Enter Bethany Mauger. From our first conversation with Bethany to discuss her joining this project as a collaborative writer we immediately knew we wanted her on our team. Very simply, she got us. She understood what we were doing and why we were doing it. Any lingering apprehension quickly dissipated. Bethany, thank you. This book would not have happened without you.

As parents now ourselves, our appreciation and admiration for ours grow daily. To both Mom and Dad Vuolo and Mama and Pops Duggar, thank you for being the first in our lives to tell us of the hope we could hold in Christ. Your faithfulness, friendship, and love are the foundation of this story.

A very special thanks to our agent, Albert Lee. Your expertise, diligence, and commitment made a potentially very tedious task a delight. And your passion is contagious, as well as your laugh.

To the team at Worthy Books/Hachette Nashville, working with each of you has been a dream we'd rather not wake up from. Thank you to Daisy Hutton, Abigail Skinner, India Hunter, Patsy Jones, Katie Robison, Eliot Caldwell, Cat Hoort, Barbara Nelson, Jody Waldrup, Whitney

Hicks, Yasmin Mathew, and Jeff Holt. Your individual and collective brilliance has left an indelible mark.

Oh, and to Beth Adams, who is too humble to want a mention: thank you. We'd like to take this opportunity to let you know how sorry we are for the late-night texts, stupid questions (yes, they exist), and missed deadlines (note the plural). You're the best. Also, sorry for the mention.

Russell Baer: you're a magician.

It must be said: without Jeremy Fall and Aaron Ahmadi, we wouldn't be writing an acknowledgments page, because there would be no book. And to think that it all began at Carnival Restaurant in Sherman Oaks! You guys have changed our world for the better. Thank you for believing in us more than we believe in ourselves.

It's been quite a journey, our lives up until this point. We've been to the top of mountains and the dark depths of valleys. Yet through it all, "your rod and your staff, they comfort me." Our deepest gratitude is reserved for our God and Savior, the Lord Jesus Christ. For it is true what the Reverend Edward Payson once wrote, that "fame is nothing, health is nothing, life is nothing. Jesus, Jesus is all!"

About the Authors

Jinger and Jeremy Vuolo star in TLC's hit show *Counting On*. While it's challenging to stand out in a family with nineteen kids—not to mention numerous spouses and grandchildren—Jinger and Jeremy have managed to amass a large following as they live out their faith and family values. The couple's biggest blessing has been raising their daughter, Felicity, who captures the hearts of their loyal fans everywhere. Hailing from Springdale, Arkansas, Jinger is an avid home cook and a gifted pianist and violinist and uses her talents to support her mother-in-law Diana's nonprofit organization, Swan 4 Kids. Jeremy is a former professional soccer player from Downingtown, Pennsylvania, now enrolled in the graduate program at The Master's Seminary. They live in Los Angeles, California.